THE SPELLBINDER'S GIFT

The

SPELLBINDER'S

GIFT

OG MANDINO

Fawcett Columbine
New York

A Fawcett Columbine Book
Published by Ballantine Books

Copyright © 1995 by Og Mandino

Library of Congress Cataloging-in-Publication Data
Mandino, Og.
The spellbinder's gift / Og Mandino.
p.   cm.
ISBN: 0-449-90690-6
I. Title.
PS3563.A464S64   1995
813'.54—dc20   94-26383
CIP

Manufactured in the United States of America
First Edition: January 1995
10 9 8 7 6 5 4 3 2 1

For my grandson . . .
WILLIAM AUGUSTINE MANDINO
. . . another spellbinder

He ended, and a kind of spell
Upon the silent listeners fell,
His solemn manner and his words
Had touched the deep, mysterious chords,
That vibrate in each human breast alike.

—Henry Wadsworth Longfellow,
Tales of a Wayside Inn

THE SPELLBINDER'S GIFT

It was truly a relaxed and wonderful evening and well past midnight when Mary and I finally arrived home. As we were both undressing, I asked, "Well, hon, what do you think of the man?"

"Bart, he is as impressive and charming up close as he was onstage. There is a special magnetism, an aura of some sort surrounding him that's hard to explain. He's appealing and attractive and yet I caught myself lowering my voice a couple of times when I was answering his questions . . . as a child might do when speaking to an adult who represented authority. And with that handsome face and beard he reminds me of some of the figures in religious paintings in our church when I was little. He almost looks as if he should be wearing a halo."

"Mary, what are you saying?"

"Bart, I'm sorry. I'm not really sure what I'm saying."

I

🌿

For more than forty years, going back to the days when our young American boys were dying in a mysterious far-off place called Korea, *Guys and Dolls* was lighting up Broadway, cold sufferers were learning to love antihistamines, Dr. Kinsey had most of us talking openly about sex, Brando was flexing his muscles in *A Streetcar Named Desire* and we finally ended our Berlin airlift after almost 300,000 flights of mercy . . . for four memorable decades from a small second-story walk-up office not far from Times Square I had served as exclusive booking agent to many of the most famous and dynamic motivational speakers in the entire world.

And then, with little advance warning, the entire roster of uniquely talented individuals that I had developed and represented loyally for so long vanished in less than twelve months! My three oldest professional speakers decided that they had endured enough plane flights and hotel meals and would stay home, live off their fat mutual-fund portfolios and write their memoirs, another developed cancer of the throat, one had a stroke that paralyzed most of his left side and my four most in-demand and highest-priced speakers, all close friends of mine, passed away.

On that very sad and bleak February morning, after I had served as a pallbearer for the fourth time in seven months, I returned to my office both physically and emotionally drained, gathered up my most important papers and files and locked the door behind me, quite certain that my business and professional future had been buried along with the bodies of my friends. I was sixty-eight.

A year or so later I was still trying very hard to enjoy many of the activities that retirees who can afford it are usually doing to fill their hours and enrich their so-called golden years. Mary and I joined a Manhattan bridge club, played golf often during the week and even began attending movie matinees. My helpmate, bless her heart, did more than her share to make retirement for us the heaven on earth that so many dream about. We traveled, we competed in slot-machine tournaments in Reno and Atlantic City, fished in the blue waters off Bermuda, ate peanuts and drank beer at Yankee Stadium, visited scores of museums and cheered the horses and greyhounds in Florida. Still, every now and then, in the midst of some activity, the lady I had been married to for almost forty-five years would cup my face in the palms of her two tiny hands, cock her pretty head and say, "You're bored, aren't you?"

I would always shake my head, kiss her on the forehead and reply, "Of course not," but after two people have loved each other as long as we have, there's not much sense in trying to lie.

There was one activity from my pre-retirement days that I still continued to enjoy and probably needed a lot more since becoming an unemployed "couch potato," and that was jogging. Every morning at dawn, for more than thirty years, if I was in town and the weather allowed, I had always followed the same routine. I'd ease myself out of bed slowly so that I wouldn't wake Mary, climb into one of my many warm-up suits, consume a large glass of orange juice, cereal and a single cup of black coffee, make certain I had my keys, and close the door quietly as I departed.

Central Park was only two blocks west of our Park Avenue apartment, and through the years I had probably jogged over every foot of its roads, trails and pathways, alternating my course from time to time so that I could enjoy all the park's wonders from Cleopatra's Needle to Strawberry Fields, from the Belvedere Castle to Shakespeare Garden, from the Pond to the Great Lawn.

The park's eight-hundred-plus acres, set in the heart of the busiest and noisiest metropolis in the western world, was my heaven on earth, my constant refuge from all the pressures and cares of life and business. Through the years I habitually timed my run to last just about an hour, usually emerging through the Artists' Gate on Central Park South. I would then turn left, pass through the cool green area known as Grand Army Plaza, cross Fifth Avenue when the traffic lights allowed and continue jogging east for two more blocks before turning north on Park Avenue, gradually slowing my pace until I finally arrived at our apartment building.

Mary was always up by the time I returned each morning, and after I had showered, shaved and dressed, I would spend

5

some time with her and another cup of coffee before either walking or taking a cab to my office on West 44th Street, depending on what was on tap for the day. Since my retirement, however, I would usually just crawl into my blue jeans and a sports shirt, after showering and shaving, and together we would watch the morning news and "The Today Show." However, being a witness to the world in action on television while I sat passively on my duff and struggled with the morning's crossword puzzle in *The New York Times* was just not my idea of what I should be doing with the rest of my days.

And then, on a hot and humid early June morning that I shall never forget, my life suddenly took an unexpected turn. I'm not sure I understand what happened, even to this day. Someone once wrote that God seems to play chess with all of us from time to time. He will make moves on our personal chessboard of life and then sit back, waiting to see if we react, how we react and what our next move will be, if any.

"Use it while you have it!"

"Tomorrow is found only on the calendars of fools!"

"It's a lot later than you think!"

He was wearing a tattered red T-shirt and stained blue jeans and his right foot, sockless, protruded through a gash in a grimy, untied sneaker. Unkempt hair, dingy gray and streaked with yellow, hung limply below his shoulders. His large and sallow face was etched with heavy dark lines, scarred by several blotches of purple and his deep-set eyes, beneath bushy eyebrows, were bloodshot, but the voice screeching out those old maxims was strong and commanding. He was sitting in a wheelchair, dangerously close to the curb, on the sidewalk at the corner of Central Park South and Fifth Avenue. As I completed my morning in the park, saluted the statue of Simón Bolívar and turned east toward Fifth Avenue on my way home, he was directly in my path.

Central Park South and Fifth is a busy corner at almost any hour of the day, but in this morning rush period the wide sidewalk is always packed with a constant parade of briefcase-carrying men and women, one horde heading north and the other south, eyes staring straight ahead as if they were all hypnotized, pushing and scurrying as they dodge the smaller group of marchers moving east and west . . . all heading toward their own little high-rise cubicles of aggravation. As I drew closer to the noisy and frightening apparition coiled in his wheelchair, I could see that he was holding a small, tattered Bible in one gnarled fist and a metal cup in the other. To my amazement, instead of working the commuter crowd in general, he was directing his hoarse words and gestures solely toward me! Hesitantly I slowed my pace as I approached and he raised his old Bible, aimed it right at my head as if it were a weapon and shouted, "Do it now! You! You! Do it now!"

He was directly in my path as I neared my Fifth Avenue crosswalk, waving toward me—me!—with both hands and yelling, "You! You must pick them today! You must pick them today! They will not be blooming tomorrow! They never bloom tomorrow!" Even a few sophisticated commuters were now beginning to slow down and stare.

Rarely in my life, if ever, have I tried to avoid confrontations of any sort. But this time, instead of jogging right past my frightening wheelchair counselor and continuing on home for a nice warm shower, I made a sudden right turn when I was only a few yards in front of him, dashed across Central Park

South with the rushing crowd and the green light and continued jogging south on Fifth Avenue's busy sidewalk—away
from the wheelchair—and very definitely in the opposite direction from my northern route home!

I still don't understand what happened that morning but
not once . . . not once in the next twenty minutes or so, as I
continued on my southerly course, did I ask myself what the
hell I was doing or where I thought I was going or why I wasn't
heading north instead of south. I just kept jogging along, at my
usual Central Park pace, like some sort of puppet on a string as
I moved past old familiar landmarks—Bergdorf Goodman,
Tiffany, I. Miller, the Crown Building, Corning Glass, the
brownstone Fifth Avenue Presbyterian Church, Gucci's, the
St. Regis Hotel, Cartier and St. Patrick's Cathedral.

Finally I slowed to a walk, turned right off Fifth Avenue and
continued west for another two blocks before pausing, slightly
out of breath, to lean against a rusted green lightpost and stare
down West 44th Street's final dingy block before it emptied
into Times Square, the very same block where for four decades
I had presided over one of the most profitable and unusual talent agencies in the world.

Now I was walking west toward Times Square . . . slowly,
very slowly, almost as if I were in some sort of trance. I moved
carefully over the cracked, pitted and litter-strewn sidewalk
while two snarling lanes of one-way traffic, primarily cabs and
delivery trucks spewing foul-smelling fumes, roared eastward
as their drivers leaned on their horns, causing crescendoes of
frightening sound to wash off the old stone buildings in wave
after wave.

Halfway down the street I stopped and turned until I was

facing the buildings on the north side of the noisy and busy thoroughfare. I stared to my left at the old, mottled Savoy marquee and the nearby garish yellow sign above a store entrance proclaiming DELI GROCERY in bright red. Then there was the Cafe Un Deux Trois with its red awning extending almost to the curb, a cozy spot where I had dined with clients, talent and friends for so many years. Adjoining the restaurant was the famed Belasco Theatre, built by David Belasco in 1907 and the home of countless unforgettable theater experiences for New Yorkers and the world through so many seasons. Now signs that were stained and dingy hung from the once-famous marquee of the empty theater, suggesting that one should see a Broadway show "just for the fun of it" and displaying a telephone number that one could call for tickets. How sad.

At last I finally summoned up enough courage to turn my head to the left of the Belasco and ran my eyes along the second-story row of windows until I saw it—and to me it looked as good as any painting of Raphael's! On one window, in gold leaf and still very legible, were the words MOTIVATORS UNLIMITED and painted on the window to its right was my name, also in caps, BART MANNING, PRES. On the bottom portion of the first window was an air conditioner but on the other, also in gold leaf, were the words WE MOVE THE WORLD WITH THE SPOKEN WORD!

As I stared up at those grimy pieces of framed glass, the center of my universe for so long, my vision suddenly became very blurred. I reached down, tapped the pocket of my warm-up suit, felt my keys and, as soon as there was a break in the traffic, dashed across the street to an old, familiar street-level metal door almost blocked from view by carts and dollies filled with boxes of all sizes that were being unloaded from a huge red truck. I inserted my key in the lock, as I had done thousands of times over the years, and leaned against the gray, pitted frame until it finally swung inward with a loud groan. I raced up the stairway.

What was I doing here? Instead of being in our cozy apartment, watching the morning news with Mary, why had I returned, after more than a year, to the familiar scene of so much personal success and triumph when I had already closed the book on those chapters of my life? Had God made a move on *my* chessboard of life this morning? That screaming ruffian in his wheelchair, blocking my path home, was he part of some design far beyond my comprehension that had forced me to turn south on Fifth Avenue? Or was I now about to open the door to my old office simply because I had been dreaming about a return visit for many months? Had God really made a move? If so, I had absolutely no idea what I was supposed to do about it.

Still . . . it was *my* move now.

II

❦

I sat tensely in the familiar old and worn leather-covered armchair for probably thirty minutes, trying to gather my thoughts, elbows resting on the faded burgundy blotter that lay on top of my dusty, oversized oak desk. Finally, after taking several deep breaths, I reached hesitantly for the telephone, removed the receiver from its cradle and hit the buttons seven times.

Almost instantly I heard Mary's voice . . . "Hello?"

"Hi . . . it's me."

Her words were clipped and icy. "Where are you?"

"I'm . . . I'm at the old office, sitting at that great desk you gave me for my fortieth birthday. Remember? Seems like only yesterday to me."

Now I could hear her sobbing. "What the hell is wrong with you, Bart? When did we start having secrets from each other? Why didn't you tell me, for God's sake, that you weren't planning to come right home today, as you always do, after your

run in the park? I've been sitting here, next to the phone, saying every prayer I know and imagining all sorts of terrible
things like you in some emergency room with a heart attack.
And where are you . . . ?"

"I told you. I'm at the office."

"Wrong. You don't have an office anymore, dear husband of
mine. Don't you remember? You retired more than a year ago!
You're even collecting social security checks now!"

I hesitated. "Sorry, hon. Truly I am. I don't know what to
say. Mary, you must believe me, I don't understand what happened and I surer than hell had no secret plans to come here
today, either when I left our apartment or after I finished my
jog through the park. And I have no idea what I'm supposed
to be doing here . . . now that I'm here. Maybe I'm starting to
lose it. Maybe the old mind is finally beginning to go."

"Bart, please . . . this is your wife you're talking to. I've
watched that wonderful head of yours function efficiently and
successfully for a lot of years. It seemed to be running just fine
yesterday when you were going over our investments with me.
Now—now you'd like me to believe that you have no expla-
nation for how or why you traveled all the way . . . all the way
. . . from Central Park to West Forty-fourth . . . seventeen or
eighteen blocks in the opposite direction from our apartment
. . . when all the time you had been planning to come directly
home to me? Please! Please, dear, why not just face the truth
and admit it . . . at least to me and especially to yourself . . .
that it was only a question of time before you returned to your
old bookie joint?"

"Bookie joint" was Mary's pet name for my office, since it
was from there, she had very proudly told a *Variety* reporter

long ago, that her husband booked the thoroughbreds of the speaking profession and then cashed in on their winning performances, day after day, year after year.

"Husband of mine," Mary continued in a voice one would use to talk to a young child, "how long has it been since you functioned in your professional capacity as an agent from that address?"

"Fourteen months or so, I guess."

"How about the rent? You're not occupying those quarters any longer but are we still paying the rent on that place?"

"Mary," I sighed, feeling very foolish, "you know we are. You write all the checks, as you've always done. You also know that we've still got several large file cabinets here, filled with a lot of important papers. There are also six or seven big cardboard cartons of memorabilia piled up in these two rooms plus scores of framed autographed photos that we just haven't been able to find a decent place to store."

"Face it, Bart. We never looked very long or very hard. There are plenty of safe self-storage facilities right here in Manhattan and you know it. Now, how about that telephone you're holding right now to talk with me. Must be quite dusty. Until today, it probably hasn't been used since you closed up shop but we're still sending a check to NYNEX every month, are we not?"

"Yes."

"Is that big brass lamp still sitting on your desk?"

"It's still here. On the far left corner, where it's always been."

I turned the switch above its base and the room was filled with warm light.

"Is the lamp turned on, Bart?"

"It is now. Working fine."

"It had better be, because I've also been mailing Con Edison a check every month without fail, just as you asked me to do. Remember?"

I was beginning to feel very foolish and could think of nothing to say that made any sense at all. My old celebrity friends, in their framed black-and-white glossy photographs autographed to me, hanging on the wall to the left of my desk, all seemed to be staring directly at me now. Spencer Tracy, Adlai Stevenson, Napoleon Hill, Billy Rose, Edward R. Murrow, Dale Carnegie, Judy Garland, Norman Vincent Peale, Elsa Maxwell, Elmer Wheeler, Cavett Robert, Fritz Kreisler, Bruce Barton, Jackie Gleason—all of them, even those who were smiling, appeared to be watching me with anxiety and, yes, a touch of pity.

"Bart?" Her voice had lost its frigid edge.

"Yes, hon?"

"Since your retirement, have you been in that office even once before today?"

"I swear . . . I have not."

I heard the sigh. "I believe you. Now, please listen to me. Stay there awhile and do some thinking . . . about yourself . . . about us . . . about the rest of your life. Maybe you should even think about getting back into the business. I've always felt that you were one of those Type A characters who are never happy unless they're always busy. Look at our old friend, Dr. Peale. He's over ninety but he's still flying around the country giving several speeches a month and loving it. Remember at that cocktail party for the governor, when I asked Norman why he was still making speeches and writing books instead of just taking life easy with Ruth at their farm? He said that although he had written more than forty books on positive thinking he was afraid there were still a few negative thinkers in our country and so he still had some unfinished work. If he can continue doing his thing at his age, I guess there's no reason, if you really want to, why you can't return to your desk with that phone to your ear and do exactly what you've done so well in the past—book speakers."

"Have you forgotten, lady? I don't have any speakers to book anymore. They're all either retired or dead."

"Okay, so sit back now, at that old desk, relax and think about all of this. Bart, you know you haven't been happy, really happy, since the day you locked that office door and walked away. You're not the same man I was married to for so long, and I'd kinda like to have that other guy back in my life, even if it means that he has to unretire himself and get back in the rat race, so that I have to start sharing him again with the gang at Lindy's. If that will make you happy, then I'll be happy!"

"And the talent? Where do I find them?"

"As if you don't know. First, there's the Rostrum Professionals of America that you only helped to found and organize more than thirty years ago. I'm pretty sure I sent a check, at your request, renewing your membership for another year, back in the spring. It seems to me that we received a large packet from them, in just the last week or so, announcing details of this year's annual convention in Washington, D.C., sometime in July, as I recall. Wow, I can just imagine the mob scenes if word ever got around, at the convention, that the legendary agent, Bart Manning, was present and scouting for new talent to handle. I'd have to come with you just to be your bodyguard, like the old days, remember?"

"Sure do. We had a lot of fun, didn't we? Of course, find-ing a few new good speakers, as damn hard as that would be, is only half the challenge. Then we'd have to keep them happy by booking enough speaking dates for each of them which would take a lot of time and effort and I haven't even talked with a single meeting planner for over a year. I don't know. . . ."

"Bart, just a phone call from you to let them know you're back in business would be all that is necessary, and you know it."

"I love you!"

"And I love you. Call me before you leave the office, please."

"You mean . . . like always?"

"Like always."

I placed the receiver gently back on its cradle, rose and walked over to the grimy window looking out on West Forty-fourth. How many times, through the years, had I stood in this same spot, turning some business problem over in my mind, while every conceivable classification of human being and ve-hicle passed before me on the street below?

I turned, stepped around two large, bulging cartons and walked into the smaller anteroom. There were still several sheets of correspondence in Grace Samuels's in-basket, but her typewriter was covered and all her pens and pencils were neatly stacked in a square holder along with pads of Post-it notes. "Amazing Grace" I had always called her, and I meant it; no one had ever been blessed with a better assistant. She had gone through a terrible time trying to deal with my closing the agency. I wondered how she was doing. Last time we had spoken, on the telephone months ago, she said that she still hadn't taken on a steady job since she hadn't been able to find another boss like me. Bless her.

I walked around to the back of Grace's desk and stood close to what she had always referred to as our altar, photographs of many of the speakers we had represented in the past. At the very center, in a heavy gold frame, was a sepia-tinted print of Eric Champion, that very special man who had changed my life forever. After playing very tiny roles in several Broadway productions following my discharge from the service in 1945, I had finally grown tired of going hungry and landed a regular-paying job in the offices of the William Morris Agency. In a little more than a year they had managed to knock enough of the rough edges off me so that I was beginning to deal with some of the lower-priced talent they represented as well as meeting planners and nightclub and hotel people.

I worked long hours and loved it. One evening, late in January, I didn't leave the office until well past nine. The Manhattan streets were almost deserted. Two blocks from my apartment, as I turned a corner, I came upon the first mugging of my life. The victim was sprawled on the snowy sidewalk, his body twisting violently as his assailant lifted some sort of club over his head. I leapt on the attacker's back without even thinking. We rolled over together twice on the cold cement before he pulled loose from my grasp, struggled to his feet and ran off into the darkness. Within minutes two police cruisers appeared and the well-dressed man with white hair who had been attacked had staggered to his feet, his head bleeding badly as he repeated to me, again and again, "Thank you, son . . . thank you, son. God bless you! God bless you! Thank you."

I gave the police my name and address and after I assured them that I needed no medical attention I continued on my way home, hearing the sound of an approaching ambulance's siren just as I unlocked my front apartment door.

I had almost forgotten the incident until, two weeks later, the phone rang in my little office. When I lifted the receiver I heard Lucy, our receptionist, telling me that a Mr. Eric Champion wanted to see me. I started to tell her that I didn't know any Eric Champion, when she said, "He says you saved his life on the streets a couple of weeks ago. Did you, Bart?"

"I don't know. Okay, send him on back."

Tom Murphy, another William Morris trainee sharing the small room with me, leaned across his desk, frowning, and asked, "Did I hear you say Eric Champion?"

I nodded.

"Don't you know who Eric Champion is, Bart?"

"Never heard of him."

Tom shook his head in mock wonder at my ignorance. "Eric Champion, my friend, is probably one of the highest, if not the highest-paid inspirational and motivational speaker—I guess that's what they're called—in the country! Here at William Morris we concentrate most of our efforts on show business talent, but I've got to tell you, I heard this man speak at the Garden about a year ago and the place was packed. He's really something! In his own category of talent I'll bet he's as big as Crosby and Gable are in theirs."

My impeccably dressed visitor was already removing his light cashmere overcoat and dark blue scarf as he walked down the narrow hall toward me, smiling and extending his hand as he drew closer. "The police were kind enough to give me your address, Mr. Manning, and then your landlady told me where you worked. I just wanted to stop by and thank you again for what you did to save me from that monster. Who knows, I may even owe you my life."

"I'm just glad I happened to come along when I did, sir. You feeling okay, now?"

"Feel just fine, thank you. Had to cancel only one speaking engagement, and the nasty gash on my head is already starting to heal. Tell me, how long have you been with William Morris?"

"A little more than a year. I've still got an awful lot to learn."

"Do you enjoy the work?"

"Hate all the paper shuffling and the legal stuff involved with contracts and bookings but I love working with clients and trying to provide them with the right kind of talent for their club or hotel or convention. I think I'm going to be good at it if the big boys are patient with me."

"I'm sure they will be. They're a fine organization. They've wanted to handle my bookings for the past several years, but my wife, Martha, was attending to all of that and she was very competent. Plus she loved the work. She . . . she . . . passed away just before Christmas."

"I'm so sorry, sir."

He raised his hand and closed his eyes. "Life goes on. I just had to thank you, once again, for being my savior in the dark.

I'll never forget it. Let's have dinner some night. It's the very least I can do to show my gratitude. I'll call you. What's your home phone number?"

Our first dinner together led to another and then another and gradually we grew very close. Although Eric Champion was old enough to be my father, our friendship ripened until one day, at lunch, he made me a proposal that I could not possibly refuse. He offered to lend me ten thousand dollars, interest free, that I could pay back whenever I was able. With that money I was to open my own agency, hire a secretary, rent office space and commence booking all of his speeches. He would give me his files and contracts involving future engagements already booked as well as names of his clients and companies to whom he had given speeches in the past. I was to receive a commission of twenty-five percent of his speaking fee for every booking I made which, forty years ago, in his special case, was a rare but very firm $2,000. News that I was handling Mr. Champion, he assured me, would spread quickly throughout the speakers "grapevine" and I undoubtedly would receive many queries from other speakers regarding the possibility of my representing them. Also, as time passed, Champion promised, most of the corporate meeting planners would learn of his new affiliation and they would be contacting me, especially after we did a mailing to everyone. We sealed our deal with a handshake. And so, Motivators Unlimited, in the spring of 1950, opened its tiny and unpretentious office on West 44th Street and the rest, as they are always saying, is history.

Now I reached for Eric's framed photograph, hanging on the wall of many, and placed the palm of my hand gently and lovingly over his classic face. For more than thirty wonderful years I had booked every one of his speeches until, one night, in the summer of 1984, he dropped dead at the lectern while waving and bowing to a standing ovation, after addressing a large group of Texas cattle ranchers in a Dallas hotel ballroom. "How appropriate," sobbed Grace when we received the shocking news, "that he should die in Texas with his boots on."

During my career as an agent, I never booked an actor, actress, singer, musician or music group of any sort. I purposely limited myself to handling only that rare and hard-to-define individual who had both the reputation and the rare ability to deliver a stirring motivational and inspirational speech filled with facts and observations from his or her own personal experiences. My clients were usually leading corporations who were seeking that special person to give their annual convention some additional luster as well as a much-needed positive and dynamic keynote address.

Through the years, many talented individuals joined Eric and myself to make Motivators Unlimited the great success that it was, and most of their photos surrounded his on that special wall of personalities that Grace had assembled so lovingly. Now I stepped back, turning slowly—and sadly—away from the photographs. What a great group! We had all worked so well together and had been, in the best of terms, family.

I lowered myself into the chair behind Grace's desk, picked up her phone and dialed her number.

"Hello . . ."

"Hello, you . . ."

"Bart? Bart, is that you?"

"Guilty. Guess where I am, lady."

"Oh, God, I don't know. Are you all right?"

"I'm fine . . . and I'm sitting in your seat . . . at your desk."

"In our office?" she screamed.

"You've got it."

"Bart, what are you up to?"

"How would you like to come back to work?"

There was no reply. I waited. Finally I said, "Grace, are you still there?"

"I'm here. My heart was beating too damn fast to talk. Are you serious? I don't know what's happening and I don't care, but I'd love to come back. When shall I start?"

"Still have your office key?"

"Of course."

"Okay . . . your first two assignments—"

"Shoot!"

"Please call one of your old friends at our esteemed Rostrum Professionals of America, find out when and where their national convention is and make all the necessary reservations for both Mary and myself, convention, hotel and airlines, okay?"

"No problem. I've done that a few times in my career. What else?"

"See if you can get someone to come in here to vacuum, clean and dust and make sure they do the windows. They're filthy."

"How soon?"

Grace's apartment was on West 48th Street, only ten minutes away, and so I knew it wouldn't take her very long to get into action. "As soon as possible," I replied.

"And when do you want me to start?"

"You already have, special lady."

After hanging up I just sat there, the fingers of both hands clasped tightly together, my eyes closed. I was trembling.

"Well, God," I whispered softly, "now it's your move again."

III

❦

Our scowling long-haired cabbie in his frayed New York Mets T-shirt with his impossible-to-pronounce Middle Eastern name glaring back at us from his dash-mounted taxi permit did his valiant best to get us to LaGuardia Airport in time for our flight despite a steady downpour that made Manhattan's morning traffic just a little better than complete gridlock. We had just ten minutes to spare when we finally boarded Delta's Flight 1747 which took off exactly at 9:30 A.M. bound for Washington's National Airport. As always, Mary held my hand tightly during takeoff, and at last we were on our way to the nation's capital to attend our first speakers convention in five years.

"The Omni Shoreham Hotel," she sighed wistfully as the plane continued its noisy climb. "Remember that special night there, Bart?"

I squeezed her hand gently. "It already seems like a lifetime ago, hon . . . 1961 . . . JFK's inaugural ball."

Mary nodded and smiled. "There we were, all decked out in tux and evening gown, nervously pacing the lobby of our Georgetown hotel along with several other couples who were also heading for the ball while the wet snow, already more than a foot deep outside, continued to fall. The hotel people kept telling us that Washington was almost completely shut down and all streets were impassable."

"What made it so frustrating," I said, "was that the Omni was only a mile or so away and yet we might as well have been in Los Angeles for all the good it did us."

"I remember, hon, that after a couple of agonizing hours of waiting in vain for a cab we finally went back upstairs to our room and I just threw myself on the bed and began to bawl in frustration."

"That didn't last long. After ten minutes or so, as I remember, you jumped up, wiped away your tears, went into the bathroom, freshened up . . . and then we went back down to the lobby to try again, reasoning that if we were being marooned by the snow, everyone else trying to get to the inaugural ball probably had the same problem."

"Bart, I'll never forget the look on your face when, after another hour or so of agonized waiting, the hotel doorman finally produced a cab for us and two other couples and the driver announced, when we were all crowded into the taxi, that the fare would be a hundred dollars per couple—for the one-mile trip. You never even uttered a single cuss word, just nodded. I was very proud of you."

"I was very proud of me, too. But it was all worth it. When we finally checked our coats and edged our way into that packed Regency Ballroom and saw our new president and his pretty young wife on the ballroom floor alone, dancing cheek to cheek . . ."

". . . to 'Moon River.' "

"You even remember the song they were playing?"

She nodded proudly. "It was very precious and at least for a few hours we were all a tiny part of Camelot. What a nice memory."

I reached down for my scuffed and scratched old Samsonite black leather attaché case which I had placed, for takeoff, under the seat in front of me.

"The great Bart Manning's security blanket," Mary sighed as she reached over and caressed the faded leather.

"You're right. I would never go on a business trip or even to a meeting in the city without this."

"And where has it been stashed for the past year or so?"

"It was in the old office, on the floor next to my desk, right where I had left it, waiting to be lured out of retirement."

"Maybe it's time you got yourself a nice new one if you plan to do much traveling."

"Never! When the time comes, you can bury us together."

I snapped open the frayed case and removed several colorful promotional pieces that Grace had just received from our speakers association headquarters in Denver. They described in glowing terms the seemingly endless array of lectures, celebrity speakers and mini-seminars covering just about every facet of the speaking profession that would be available to attendees during the coming four full days and evenings of the thirty-fourth annual convention of the Rostrum Professionals of America. I handed a program to Mary, who frowned and asked, "What am I supposed to do with this?"

"Help me . . . as you did in the old days. Look through the pages and see if any of the speakers making presentations might be someone I'd be interested in. You know my kind of speaker. I don't care about any of the so-called experts on sales or time management or negotiating or whatever is hot this season. I want someone with charisma and that special ability to walk up to a lectern and grab any audience until you can't hear a sound in the auditorium except breathing."

"Okay, fella, I'll do it providing you don't ask me to sit with you and rate these people in person like we used to do. I'm planning to get in some real serious shopping once we're settled in at the Omni. Was hoping that a few of our old friends would be at the convention and while you guys attended the sessions, we gals could take off and spend some of your money like the old days."

After a silent quarter hour or so, Mary closed her convention program and tapped me on the knee with it. "Bart, this speakers contest sounds intriguing," she said as she removed a single glossy white sheet from her program. "Something new and different. Can't remember anything like this ever being done before. Years ago the board wouldn't even have considered such a thing."

I had no idea what she was talking about. "Mary, I don't have that page in my program. Tell me about it."

"You've heard of Ted & Margaret's Frozen Dinners?"

"Of course."

"What's their motto?"

I didn't even hesitate. "Our taste speaks for itself."

"Very good. Well, apparently the people in Ted & Margaret's marketing department decided that, after so many years, just having the taste of their product speak for itself was not enough in a field that now has so much competition. Borrowing from the theme of their motto, they have now decided to have the finest orator they can find speak for the taste of their product, so they are conducting a contest at our convention to discover a World Champion of the Lectern. Apparently each of our association's six regions has been having elimination contests to select the finest speaker in its area, and these six will compete on the last afternoon of our convention to determine the nation's best. Each speech is to be no more than twenty minutes in length on any subject, and the contestants will be judged by a panel of impartial judges selected by the corporation."

"And the winner gets . . . ?"

"A large trophy proclaiming that he or she is this year's World Champion of the Lectern as well as being honored by the association. He or she, of course, will also have a picnic preparing new promotion material informing prospective clients that now they can book the very best, if they wish. There's more. . . ."

"Shoot!"

"The winner will get to do nine television commercials, one of which will be run nationally each month, beginning in September. For that little chore, he or she will receive a quarter of a million dollars. What seems so strange to me, Bart," she said as she handed me the speakers contest page, "is that all six finalists are completely unfamiliar to me. And to think that there was a time when we knew just about everyone by name who attended these conventions. I guess we've been away too long. Take a look."

I studied the photos and brief bios of each contestant and shook my head. "Me too. Don't recognize anyone. But then, let's face it, we don't even recognize very many of the new breed of movie stars. Our old world keeps changing, but it doesn't seem to be making much progress. I can't believe that we'll never again see a Sears catalogue or that IBM is struggling or that we still have ten million unemployed or that we're now giving out condoms in high school. No wonder the Eric Champions we knew have all left us for a better place."

Mary patted my knee gently. "Tell you what, husband. On Thursday I won't shop. We'll go to the speakers contest together to check out those six finalists. Okay?"

"You've got a date!"

IV

Through the years, Eric Champion and several of my other speakers had frequently addressed large groups and conventions at the Omni Shoreham in our nation's capital. Few hotels could even come close to matching the lustrous history of the sixty-year-old Omni, and as Mary and I sat in our suite, after a light room-service lunch, we both became fascinated by the material about the hotel's past that we found on one of the large mahogany dressers. I'm sure that we acted and sounded more like awe-struck teenagers than experienced travelers as we began to share interesting tidbits of information about the hotel with each other.

"Did you know, hon," Mary exclaimed, "that every president since Franklin Roosevelt has held an inaugural ball here?"

"I did, because I remember Eric telling me that the hotel had offered to build a special ramp and elevator for Mr. Roosevelt and his wheelchair after he won his first election and that established a precedent that's still alive. Inaugural balls are now always held in the Omni's Regency Ballroom. I can still remember how excited Eric was when he was booked by the American Medical Association to speak in that same room for the first time."

"Bart, listen to this," she said, waving one of the hotel's brochures. "Would you believe that Harry Truman had private poker games here while he was president? Room D-106 was the favorite room where he and his buddies gathered while his limousine was always parked just outside to rush him back to the Oval Office."

"Anything there about the old Blue Room?"

"I was just coming to it. Says that in the thirties and forties the hotel's Blue Room featured some of the greatest figures in the entertainment world. Now hear this! For the grand opening of the hotel in 1930, Rudy Vallee, then America's number-one crooner, flew from New York with his orchestra for the opening in an Amelia Earhart tri-motored airplane! Judy Garland, Maurice Chevalier, Marlene Dietrich, Frank Sinatra, Lena Horne and Bob Hope were only a few of the big names who performed in that room, and there is a large metal plaque just outside its doors with the name of every celebrity who has appeared there, from Edie Adams to Gretchen Wyler. It says here that the hotel liked to boast that the Blue Room converted Washington from 'a strictly Saturday-night town' to a place where dinner, dancing and entertainment were popular every evening. I've got to see that room, Bart!"

"I think it's just a large and lovely meeting room now."

"I don't care. I still want to see it. Apparently when JFK was courting Jacqueline he often took her there. What a very special hotel, Bart! I can't believe that in all our travels you and I have never come here before. Listen to this . . . just before his inaugural in January 1969, President Nixon made history here by introducing his entire cabinet-to-be over network television at a special dinner in the Diplomat Room."

"Mary, I can remember Eric telling me that during World War II, this hotel bought the entire stock of a Scottish distillery, so they were one of the few hotels serving good scotch all during the war. He also told me that they converted their riding stable into a chicken ranch, as a wartime measure, and raised thousands of broilers for their restaurants' tables."

"Tell you what, Bart. Why don't you muscle our suitcases up onto our bed and I'll unpack us as usual while you go down to the lobby and sign us in for the convention or whatever you have to do. Knowing you, I'm pretty sure you'll get involved in lots of chats and hugs as you renew old friendships—but just do me a favor and don't forget you've got a wife up here. Come back and get me in an hour or so and we can explore the hotel together. That will still give us enough time to get out of these jeans and into something a little more presentable for the opening reception."

"When does that start?"

Mary opened her convention program. "Six-thirty. There's nothing scheduled after that tonight. Maybe we'll get lucky and find some of the old gang. Then we can all go to the Garden Court, which sounds pretty nice, have a couple of drinks and tell lies like the old days."

Registration took only a few minutes. Beneath a bright yellow banner reading ROSTRUM PROFESSIONALS OF AMERICA, several young ladies were sitting primly, pen in hand, waiting. I approached the petite blonde who was sitting behind the G to M sign. She gave me her best welcome smile and I said, "Manning . . . Bart Manning and Mary."

The young lady said, "Welcome to the convention, sir." Then she ran her tiny hand down her list and nodded, handing me a registration form and ballpoint pen.

When I returned the completed registration blank to her, she handed me two large white envelopes. "One for you and one for Mrs. Manning, sir. In there you'll find all the convention information you'll need to have a great four days. And here are the nameplates for both you and your wife."

As she was handing me the small red-bordered, rectangular metal plates, she did a double take, frowned and looked closer at the top plate. Beneath my name was a brief line that read MEMBER, 35 YEARS.

"You've belonged to this association for thirty-five years, sir? Good Lord!"

I grinned and nodded. "Yes, I helped to found it. Long before you were born. How many do we have registered, do you know?"

"I heard someone say nearly two thousand."

"Well, counting our spouses, there were only twenty-six of us at the Brown Palace in Denver for our very first convention. I guess we've grown quite a bit since then, wouldn't you say?"

The young lady, now very wide-eyed, merely nodded.

"Bart! Bart Manning, is it really you? God, what a surprise!"

I spun around, recognized him immediately, inhaled deeply and yelled, "Jay! Old buddy! Boy is it good to see you!"

No handshake. Just big hugs. Then I stepped back to take a

good look at Jay Bridges, an old friend whom I hadn't seen since my last convention. Standing very erect in his tailored houndstooth checked suit with vest, every silver hair perfectly in place crowning a well-tanned and almost wrinkle-free face, he looked exactly as I remembered him.

"You old rascal," I shouted. "How marvelous you look and still so damn young. Have you discovered the fountain of youth? Wow!"

He cocked his head. "You were always a great BS man, Bart Manning. You look wonderful, too, but what the hell are you doing here? I heard you were out of the business."

"I was. Retired over a year ago but I'm thinking seriously about unretiring myself. I've missed all the aggravation and pressure. Just here to do a little talent scouting. How about you? Still charming all those ladies at their cosmetic conventions?"

He nodded. "I'm still having too much fun to quit, Bart. We've sure missed you, guy. How long has it been?"

"Haven't come for five years. Last one was in Vegas, remember?"

"I certainly do. You and I stayed up all night at Caesars, playing baccarat. We both lost a ton. And how's Mary?"

"Great. She's up in our room putting our clothes away. Jay, she'll be so damn happy to see you. You were always one of her favorite people and she kept hoping and hoping that someday I'd be your agent. How's Phyllis?"

"I buried Phyllis three years ago, Bart. Cancer."

"Jay, I'm so sorry. I didn't—"

He nodded and asked, "Hey, have you got any time?"

"Mary gave me an hour of freedom."

He took my arm. "Well, let's you and I go have a drink for old time's sake."

During most of the sixties, Jay Bridges was one of the most popular news commentators on New York radio before he wrote a hilariously funny book called *Sex à La Carte* which was considered shocking back then but wouldn't even raise an eyebrow on anyone's maiden aunt today. When the book, to everyone's surprise including the publisher's, became a smash best seller, Jay began accepting invitations to speak, first solely around Manhattan but soon before groups across the country. He made so much money that he finally resigned his position at the radio station. He never wrote another book but did manage to earn a fine living for himself for the past thirty years or so, delivering a hilarious talk on the never completely understood and constantly changing relationship between men and women. Early in his speaking career I had tried to sign him, especially after hearing him almost destroy a huge audience at the Hotel Astor, but the very capable agent who had represented him in his radio years continued to handle him very well during his platform career.

Now Jay guided me through the crowded main lobby, down into the Garden Court Lounge, through the lounge and veranda to the outside terrace with its tables shaded by huge umbrellas. We sat and ordered drinks. Behind us, hidden by a tall, trimmed hedge, we could hear laughter, shouts and splashes from the hotel's two swimming pools while the repeating sound of tennis balls crashing against racquets came from tennis courts to our left.

Jay pointed to the center of the cement courtyard area, where a large section, almost in the shape of a full circle, was painted green. "There was a huge hydraulic stage right there, Bart, and it was used to raise those big bands of our era such as Dorsey and Miller and Goodman so that the musicians played above the crowds while they danced under the stars. Funny isn't it, that with all this hotel has to offer, we have never before held our convention here."

I nodded but said nothing, feeling completely relaxed and at peace with the world as I took a long sip from my Cutty and water. Jay pushed his glass to the side, cocked his head in my direction and said, "Now tell me the truth, my dear friend of so many years, what the hell are you doing here?"

Knowing he would not be satisfied with any flip, hasty, off-the-cuff reply, I slowly and painfully gave Jay all the details of how my agency, in a year or so, lost every one of its speakers to death or retirement.

"There was no one left to book, Jay, and since I hadn't devoted the time and effort I should have in constantly looking for new talent to replace any loss of the old boys, I paid the price. Agency out of business. As you know, I had even stopped coming to our own convention to scout out the new bunch."

He smiled. "So what happened? Mary get tired of telling you that while she married you for better or worse she didn't marry you for twenty-four hours a day under her feet? What are you doing back here? God knows you don't need the money."

I was so tempted to tell him about that strange chain of events that had commenced with my morning jog out of Central Park and my confrontation with that curious, ranting soul in his wheelchair, followed by my mysterious jog south to my old office, but I couldn't, I just couldn't.

"Jay, I'm too young and healthy to waste my years sitting at home with a television remote control in my hand while I flip from "Barnaby Jones" reruns to "Days of Our Lives." I always felt that I was contributing a little something to make our world a better place when I sent a great motivational speaker to address a group and help them to realize what great miracles they really are. You were the only person I ever tried to sign up who didn't do a motivational or inspirational talk."

"You know, Bart," Jay sighed, studying the palms of his hands, "I've often wondered how well you and I would have done together."

"We'd have made a lot of money, that's for sure. Who's doing your bookings now?"

"No change. Sam Rapkin and I have now been together for almost thirty-two years. He's a good man."

I nodded in agreement. "Well, I'm going to scout around for four days and see what I can find. Wouldn't mind if I just handled one or two speakers to start over with and then I'd see how it went."

Three times, as Jay and I sat and talked, we were interrupted by individuals wearing convention badges. Each time they knew my name and who I was and said they just wanted to say hello and were honored to meet me. Feeling a little embarrassed, I would then introduce the stranger to Jay.

"Bart," Jay said, "you are without a doubt the most admired and respected agent in this whole damn business. Almost every speaker at this convention would just about kill to be handled by you. Your problem is going to be keeping a low enough profile so that you can check the performers out without being constantly hounded. How would you like me to run interference for you during the next couple of days?"

"I'd love it. Are you sure you want to do it?"

"It'd be a ball and I'd get to spend all that precious time with the great and famous Bart Manning."

I grasped his hand. "Thank you!"

He grinned. "Don't thank me. I'll be having all the fun just being your guide and bodyguard. However, there's one thing I must tell you right now, even before the hunt begins."

"What's that?"

"I don't believe you will discover anyone here as good as your Eric Champion."

I nodded and shook his hand again. "See you at the opening reception tonight, buddy?"

He shrugged his shoulders. "Where else would I go . . . without Phyllis?"

V

Still sitting at the linen-covered circular table on which room service had delivered our breakfast, I was turning the pages of USA *Today* when Mary said softly, "It was so good to see Jay and the Johnsons and the Robertsons and Anna Hubbard. Didn't realize how much I've missed the old gang."

I folded the newspaper and tossed it on the sofa. "Did you have fun?"

"I think it was a wonderful reception. Everyone, especially the hotel people, did a great job and I'm so glad it was held in the Blue Room. The three harpists scattered around the room added a nice touch, and from what I saw I do believe you really will need a bodyguard while you're here. I kept expecting someone to kneel and kiss your ring."

"Hon, I love what you said as we walked into the Blue Room last night."

"What?"

"You said, 'Bart, I'm positive we're in the right place. As

usual, whenever speakers gather, everyone is talking and no one is listening.' So, tell me, are you all set to go shopping?"

"I am. Meeting Anna Hubbard and Kay Johnson in the lobby at ten o'clock. Susie Robertson promised John she'd keep him company today, but she said she'd love to join us tomorrow if we have any money left. We told her not to worry, that we both had three Gold cards. How about you? All set?"

"I think so. Jay said he'd phone me here at nine-fifteen to find out where I'd meet him in time for the first session at nine-thirty. There are three programs going on every ninety minutes throughout the day, and Jay is letting me call my shots so that I can check out the speakers with the most potential."

"So, have you made your choice for the first one?"

I shook my head, stood, walked over to the dresser where all the convention material was stacked and picked up a program. Back at the table I opened the pages of the first day's activities and handed it to Mary. "Here, you get me started on the right foot. Maybe one of the first three caught your eye when you were looking them over on our flight. Where should I go first?"

"Okay, 'How to Tame a Tough Audience.' Presenter is John Felch from Michigan. He's one of those I did check off, come to think of it, when we were on the plane. According to this copy, his specialty is motivational and keynote speeches. He's making his presentation in the Hampton Room," she said, returning the program to me just as the phone began ringing. It was Jay.

"Break a leg!" Mary shouted as I headed for the door.

Dressed in a bright scarlet silk shirt above contrasting black pants and shoes, Jay was standing next to the Hampton Room's entrance, smiling, nodding and shaking hands as if he were running for office. "What made you select this one?" he asked, pointing toward the crowded open doorway with his thumb.

"I didn't. Mary picked it for me."

He nodded understandingly, turned and entered the noisy room. I followed. We had just located two empty seats, when a voice over the speaker system greeted us. "Ladies and gentlemen, the Rostrum Professionals of America is very proud to introduce to you one of its most dynamic and sought-after speakers discussing a subject on which he has had much experience through the years, How to Tame a Tough Audience. Let's have a warm welcome for John Felch!"

He was forty or so, and he leapt agilely up the steps of the podium despite a large, rotund body, smiling and waving until he was standing at the lectern. He pushed back a lock of black hair that had fallen across his forehead, suddenly ceased smiling and assumed an unmistakable look of fear. He cleared his throat several times and said hoarsely, "I'm very, very honored to appear before all of you today, but I realize that I am violating one of the three pieces of immortal advice given to us by Winston Churchill, who said, 'Never try to walk up a wall that's leaning towards you. Never try to kiss a person who is leaning away from you. And never speak to a group that knows more about a subject than you do.' "

Felch waited for the laughter to subside, nodding his head in appreciation, and then said, "Before I came in here this morning, my wife, Amy, and I had breakfast in that lovely Garden Court Lounge. As we were leaving she had some wise advice for me, when she saw that I was a little nervous about appearing before so many other speakers. She said, 'John, don't try to be charming, witty or intellectual. Just be yourself.'

"How do we tame a tough audience? I'll share several methods that have worked well for me, through the years, but please don't ever forget that magic ingredient called laughter as one of the best possible potions for the grouchiest grouch. Friendship and laughter are closely related. Make friends with that sea of frowning faces sitting in front of you by getting them to smile, and you will probably come away from any speech a success."

Felch paused, looking up toward the ceiling, then chuckled as if he had just thought of something funny and said, "During a recent expedition into the wildest part of darkest Africa, a group of explorers came upon a village of primitive savages. In an attempt to make friends of this very, very tough audience watching the explorers' every move, the leader of the group tried to tell the natives what it was like in the civilized, outside world.

" 'Out there,' he said, 'we love our fellow men.'

"To this the natives gave a ringing cry of 'Huzzanga!'

"Encouraged by this, the explorer continued. 'We treat others as we would want them to treat us!'

" 'Huzzanga!' exclaimed the natives with much enthusiasm.

" 'We are peaceful!' said the explorer.

" 'Huzzanga!' cried the natives.

"With a tear running down his cheek, the explorer ended

his fine speech. 'We come to you as friends, as brothers. So trust us. Open your arms to us, your homes, your hearts. What do you say?'

"The air shook with one long, mighty 'Huzzanga!'

"Greatly pleased by the reception, the leader of the explorers then began talking with the natives' chief.

" 'I see that you have cattle here,' he said. 'They are a species with which I am unfamiliar. May I inspect them?'

" 'Certainly, certainly, come right this way,' said the chief. 'But be very careful as you walk that you don't step in the huzzanga!' "

Felch nodded at the loud laughter and applause. When it had finally subsided he said, "Okay, enough of the huzzanga. Now let's zero in on some of the conditions that produce a tough audience and what we can do to make them pushovers."

On one or two occasions during the next hour I felt Jay looking at me, and when I turned he would ask softly, "Had enough?"

Each time I just shook my head. I was enjoying Felch. He had excellent platform presence, superb timing and he delivered a well-constructed talk with plenty of meat to it, without referring to a single note. Both Jay and I were among those who gave him a standing ovation when he finished.

The remainder of the morning was all downhill. One of the sessions featured a smooth-talking hustler telling us how to make a fortune on infomercials by selling packages of tapes and videos through an 800 number to lonely people sitting at home by the telephone. The other was a presentation by a heavily made-up thin woman with lavender hair extolling the virtues of publishing one's own book so that the speakers could also claim the status of an author in their promotional material . . . even a "best-selling" author, she hinted slyly. After no more than twenty minutes I nudged Jay and we retreated as quietly as we could out the door and into the Garden Court Lounge which was beginning to feel like home. We sat at the bar and ordered drinks.

"Are we having fun yet, daddy?" Jay asked after he had taken a long sip of his scotch.

"Well, we've made a start. That Felch guy from the first session has possibilities."

"Shall we continue on our talent hunt?" Jay asked.

"Oh, yes! I'm positive that somewhere among the two thousand members attending this convention I'll find one or two of my kind of speaker, the old-fashioned kind who reaches for the audiences' soul, not their wallets."

"Mr. Manning, sir . . . ?"

He was standing to my right, at the bar.

"Yes?"

"Sir, my name is Patrick Donne," he said in a deep, commanding voice as he extended a large hand toward me. "This is my first convention and when I saw you standing here I couldn't resist the temptation to at least say hello. I've admired you for many years."

"Hello," I said, shaking his hand. "Glad to meet you . . . and welcome. This is Jay Bridges, one of our very best old pros."

As they were shaking hands I couldn't help notice that three women who were sitting across the bar from us were now all staring in our direction and certainly not at Jay or me. Besides that almost hypnotic basso-profundo voice, Patrick Donne was considerably over six feet tall with wide shoulders, a sharply pointed chin covered with a light brown beard, huge brown eyes and brown hair a little too long for my taste but thankfully not long enough to be classified a ponytail.

Jay greeted the newcomer warmly, asking, "Where are you from, Patrick?"

"I'm from a little town in Montana," he grinned, "called Blessings, population less than four hundred."

"Don't imagine there's much call for public speakers in Blessings, is there?"

"No, sir," he said, smiling and shaking his head. "But there's always Billings and Bozeman and Great Falls and Helena. Actually I can get anywhere in the Northwest pretty fast in my Beechcraft."

"Oh? You fly your own plane?"

"Yes, sir. Been flying for ten years or so."

"What do you do, Pat, or is speaking full-time with you?"

"I've been speaking for about six years, Mr. Manning. I did own a pretty good size cattle ranch back there in Blessings, but this speaking began taking so much of my time, and I love it, so I decided to sell the ranch to my foreman and become full-time two years ago. Gave forty-three speeches last year, even as far away as St. Louis."

"Do you have an agent?" Jay asked casually.

"No, sir, I do it all myself."

"What do you talk on?"

"Well," he said tentatively, "the talk has been kind of changing and evolving over the years, but I'm pretty comfortable with it now. I just give my audience some rules and suggestions that have been around forever but will help anyone live a happier and more productive life. These ideas that I share with them are so obvious that the greatest mystery of all is why everyone doesn't recognize and follow them . . . so now I call my talk 'The Greatest Mystery in the World.' "

"Sounds very interesting," I replied, not quite certain what else to say. "Well, it was good to meet you. Tell me, are you enjoying your first convention?"

His large eyes opened even wider and he said, "There's almost too much to absorb. So much to take in, to learn, to remember."

I nodded. "There are some fine sessions scheduled for the next couple of days and you'll want to be sure to sit in on that very special speakers contest during the last day. You'll probably learn plenty from those six top professionals of our association when they fight it out at the lectern for a quarter of a million dollars and the world championship of our speakers profession. Don't miss that!"

Patrick Donne smiled sheepishly and stared down at the bar. "Mr. Manning, sir, I won't miss it. I'm one of the six finalists."

VI

❦

The ballroom was crowded for the association luncheon but Jay and I finally found two empty adjoining seats at a table with four speakers who I gathered were relatively new in the business. Our presence must have intimidated them a little, because, compared to the noisy tables around us, there was not much chatter as we ate until a very pretty redhead sitting directly across from me said, "Mr. Manning, I'm sure you've witnessed a long parade of professionals doing their thing through the years. Tell us who, in your opinion, were some of the very best."

Everyone at our table looked up from their plates and waited, including Jay. "That's a tough question. If by 'the very best' you mean who were masters at holding an audience in the palm of their hands, I guess I would select Rich DeVos, Amway's co-founder, Bishop Fulton J. Sheen, Bill Gove, Norman Vincent Peale, Cavett Robert, and, of course, my own very special friend, the late Eric Champion."

The redhead winced. "No women?"

"Well, you must remember that it has been only in the last ten or fifteen years that women have finally worked their way into what was pretty much an all-male profession. Now, from all I hear, there are plenty of very talented women flying around the country and appearing before huge audiences. However, I'm sorry to say that I've just never heard any of them on the platform although I'm pleased to see that this group has honored many in the past few years."

Following lunch, David Starr, a tall and handsome young man who was this year's chairman of the special awards committee, rose to explain how strict and eminently fair the process was of selecting the association's ten top professionals of the year. These speakers would join their predecessors in a very exclusive and elite group and henceforth could identify themselves on their business cards, stationery and all promotional materials as one of the very best in the business, a "Master of the Lectern."

"This year," Starr continued, "the climax to this great convention, our Thursday evening achievement dinner, will be a very memorable occasion for all of us because, for the very first time, we have an added five-star feature, approved by our officers and board of directors. Besides honoring ten new "Masters," we will also be privileged to see one of our own members crowned World Champion of the Lectern. Considering the several other fine speakers associations in this country, I need not remind you what a great honor this is for us. It will all take place right here, in this very special Regency Ballroom. Don't any of you dare miss it."

The afternoon sessions we attended produced no likely

prospects for me. We looked in on three, one titled "Who Dresses You?", another "How to Mold a New Presentation" and the third, "How to Survive a Hundred Hotels," all presented by mediocre speakers whose nervousness in front of their peers was obvious.

I've never been very good at hiding my feelings and I probably was showing my disappointment and frustration as we emerged from the Empire Room and walked through the crowded lobby. Jay slowed his pace and gripped my arm lightly. "And now, Mr. Manning, Dr. Bridges is about to give you a prescription that must be filled this evening. If anybody ever needed a change of scenery, and fast, it's you. I want you to take your lovely wife and get out of here, away from all of this. I happen to remember how much the both of you love Spanish food, so here's what I want you to do. There is a fabulous restaurant on I street called Taberna del Alabardero. Here, I'll write it down for you," he said as he scribbled on his program.

"Now, be sure to order yourself a plate of paella. It's a delicious special dish of Spanish rice. Then try the roasted duck in blueberry sauce. Go, please. Neither of you will regret it, I promise. Okay?"

I just nodded.

"Bart, what about tomorrow? Do you want to keep on with this scouting expedition?"

"Jay, I can't stop now. I've got to find what I'm looking for no matter how long it takes, and I still need your advice. I can't tell you how much your help and counsel have meant to me."

"Okay, let's meet right here by the elevator at nine-fifteen tomorrow."

I had already showered and was sitting in my robe, watching the early news on television, when Mary returned from her day at the malls, arms loaded with shopping bags. Looking very weary, she didn't accept my announcement that I was taking her out to dinner with much enthusiasm, but the day still had a happy ending. The Taberna del Alabardero was everything Jay said it was and then some, and its elegant decor was a perfect setting for one of the most delicious meals either one of us ever ate, although I passed on the roasted duck and ordered their paella de langosta, which was literally covered with lobster.

As we were entering our cab for the ride back to the Omni, I handed our young cabbie a fifty-dollar bill and asked if he would please give us a thirty-minute tour of a few Washington landmarks. He smiled and nodded, and as Mary and I held hands, in complete silence we rode slowly along the Potomac River, past the illuminated Lincoln Memorial, then the Vietnam Veterans Memorial, the Tidal Basin, serving as a perfect setting for the Jefferson Memorial, past the Washington Monument, the White House and then down Pennsylvania Avenue to the Capitol building. It is impossible for any citizen to take that ride, especially when the moon is shining down as it was, without feeling very proud to be an American.

There were tears in Mary's eyes when she stepped from the cab at the hotel. As the taxi was pulling away, she hugged me tightly and said, "Thank you, dear. That was one of the loveliest nights of my life."

"Well," I said, returning her hug, "I sure hope God lets me hang around long enough to give you a few more of them."

. . .

Wednesday's talent hunt produced no better results. After Mary and her friends headed for the shops and restaurants of Georgetown Park, Jay and I continued our search. The morning program had commenced with a general session in the Regency Ballroom featuring a presentation by an old pro, Edgar Hubbard, whom both Jay and I had known for many years. Hubbard, according to his introducer, had delivered more than three thousand speeches in the past thirty years and had received just about every honor the speaking profession could bestow. Listening to him again, after a span of many years, I remembered why I had never tried to sign him to an exclusive contract. His stage presence was magnificent, as were his gestures and delivery with a fine voice but . . . he didn't say anything! If one were just listening to any of his speeches on tape instead of enjoying his choreographic movements on the platform, one would have been bored to death. The other featured speaker was a young man in knickers, à la Payne Stewart, who walked out on the stage carrying a huge leather bag of golf clubs and proceeded to relate each club in his bag to a stage of one's life. Cute idea that might work in front of an audience of male golfers, but I wasn't so sure that a group of Mary Kay ladies would appreciate some of his humor.

Following the general session, Jay and I spent some time in two of the three concurrent presentations that followed. Nothing, not even a "maybe."

We ate most of our lunch with little talk, in the Monique Cafe. Over coffee, Jay opened his program, forced a smile and said, "Looks like some good potential prospects this afternoon, old buddy. Boy, I hope so. If we don't get lucky in the next few hours, there ain't nothing left except the speakers championship tomorrow afternoon."

During an afternoon that seemed longer than eternity, Jay and I checked out seven of the nine speakers who were being featured. We both agreed that most of them were good examples of a truly professional speaker and undoubtedly could come away from addressing most corporate gatherings with a good rating. However, I wasn't looking for just "good" speakers, I was scouting for a motivational master with stage presence, courage, charisma and a message. No one that I saw and heard even came close to fitting those tough requirements.

Mary was already back in our suite, and I guess that when I unlocked our door, I awoke her. Her shoes were off and her stockinged feet were resting on the marble coffee table. She opened her eyes as I approached and asked in a half-whisper, "Any luck, hon?"

"None. I must be getting too fussy in my old age. We just didn't see anyone that I could admire enough to want to pitch to clients. Mary, you know I can't sell them unless I really believe they're great."

"So what now?"

"Well, there is still the speaking championship tomorrow afternoon. Six of our best will each have twenty minutes in the spotlight and you promised you'd come with me, remember?"

"Bart, I wouldn't miss it for anything."

"Hon, are you okay? You look a little strange."

"I'm fine, fine . . . and I sure hope that dream I just had while I was sitting here waiting for you comes true."

"Want to tell me?"

"Sure. I must have dozed off while reading this little hotel brochure about the jogging and exercise trail in Rock Creek

Park, which I guess is just over the hill behind the Omni. Anyway, I dreamed I was jogging along, on the trail, enjoying the lush green landscape, when I suddenly noticed a small white cloud floating directly over my head, following me. Then I heard a soft voice that seemed to be coming from the cloud, saying, 'Tomorrow is the day. The heavens are about to smile on you. Do not lose hope.' Then I guess I heard you opening the door, and when I opened my eyes, you were standing there."

"What do you suppose all that means?"

"I wish I knew."

VII

❧

The Regency Ballroom was filled to capacity when association president Dick Cobden stepped from behind a golden curtain promptly at one o'clock and approached the lectern, smiling and waving. Looking from one side of the huge room to the other, he waited in silence, after raising the lectern microphone slightly, until the noisy chatter subsided.

Mary and I had wisely decided to come early and we were no more than six or seven rows from the podium, dead center. In both aisles, to our left and right but a little closer to the podium than we were, television crews fiddled with their unwieldy cameras and rolling tripods. On one camera were the initials NBC, while ABC was on the other. Mary nudged me, obviously impressed.

"Ladies and gentlemen," our association president began, "I welcome you to what I am certain will be a milestone day in the history of the Rostrum Professionals of America. The film industry has its Oscar Awards, television has its Emmys, the recording people have their Grammys and the very best writers receive Pulitzer prizes. Now, at long last, our profession is about to pay tribute to its top talent. In cooperation with Ted & Margaret's Frozen Dinners, before this day has ended we will crown the World Champion of the Lectern."

Cobden paused, nodding and smiling until the applause stopped. "Each of the six regional associations which together comprise the Rostrum Professionals of America have, during the past several months, conducted a series of contests to select the very best speaker in their region and all six winners are here today to compete in this premiere championship. Each will speak for twenty minutes, with a two-minute margin either way, on any subject of their choice. There will be a five-minute break between the first, second and third speaker, then a twenty-minute intermission followed by the final three speakers, who will be on the same time schedule—twenty minutes each, plus or minus two minutes, with a five-minute break between the fourth, fifth and sixth speaker. Four eminent individuals, selected by the marketing department of Ted & Margaret's, will be the judges. They are already seated, scattered throughout this room, and their identity is known only to the people of the corporation so no undue pressure or influence can possibly be exerted on them by any of our more zealous association members. The judges will meet in private, following the contest, to make their selection and tonight, at our closing Night of Achievement dinner, we will crown one special person World Champion of the Lectern, the very best in our profession. The corporation's co-founders, Ted and Margaret Clark, will then present that fortunate individual with a check in the amount of a quarter of a million dollars as an advance fee for nine television commercials that will be aired nationally featuring the speaker promoting their excellent products."

Cobden looked around the huge room once again, grinned and shuffled several sheets of paper. "Well," he shouted, "are we ready?"

"Yes!" the crowd roared.

"Okay. In accordance with the rules established by our officers and board of directors and the management of Ted & Margaret's Frozen Dinners, there will be no long and flowery introductions of our contestants to influence you or the judges in any way. And now, without further ado, I am most proud to present our first contestant, from Providence, Rhode Island, representing Region One . . . Sandra Bane!"

She was tall, blond and wore a pinstripe double-breasted camel-color suit. She strolled effortlessly to the lectern, acknowledging the loud applause with a warm smile and wave. Lovely woman, thirtyish, perhaps. Her smile gradually faded as she looked down at the audience and delivered none of the typical opening remarks one hears so often.

"I was a United Airlines pilot for six wonderful and exciting years and then, four years ago, following my promotion to captain, I flunked my physical. My examination disclosed that I had cancer in my right breast and so, for the following month or two, I had a new co-pilot. His name was death. We got to be pretty good friends as the days passed, and he taught me many things as I lay in my hospital bed filled with self-pity. Above all, he helped me to appreciate the special gift of each new day and to never again take that gift for granted as I had done in the past.

"Fortunately for me, the cancer had been discovered in time and two operations removed it all. After savoring the good news for a few weeks, I had to make a decision about my future. What did I really want to do with the rest of my life? Did I want to get back in the big birds? Flying was a wonderful career with a promising future and all the excitement anyone could possibly want, but the decision I finally made was the toughest I had ever made in my life . . . to come down out of the heavens and to alert others, who were probably no more grateful for the gift of each day than I had been, that the clock was ticking, and that they should seize each day, even each moment, with love and gusto and gratitude because they might not get another chance.

"And so, after many agonizing days and weeks of indecision, I hung my pilot's jacket, complete with shiny wings, in my closet, put on a business suit, wrote my first speech and, frightened to death, ventured out into the business world. I started at first just around Providence, waving my lantern and warning any group willing to listen that fulfilling their dreams and goals wasn't something that could wait for tomorrow because they had no guarantee it would ever arrive. . . ."

I turned slightly toward Mary. She never even looked at me but pushed on the tiny ballpoint pen she was holding and wrote "8" on the top of her program. I nodded in agreement.

Miss Bane's entire speech was powerful, inspirational and uplifting, and when she closed she did so on a high note of hope. The applause was long and accompanied by plenty of cheers when she finally bowed and walked off the stage.

"She's going to be tough to beat!" Mary said admiringly

when the clamor finally subsided and our association president returned to the lectern.

"Ladies and gentlemen, those talented six who are now competing for the title of World Champion of the Lectern attended a private breakfast this morning with our board, our officers and the marketing people from Ted & Margaret's Frozen Dinners, and a drawing was conducted to determine the order of our speakers' appearances this afternoon, in fairness to all of them. And so, according to the luck of the draw, the second speaker I am honored to present to all of you is from Phoenix, Arizona, representing the Southwest, Region Five . . . Jo Jo Smith!"

He looked more like a dapper Washington lobbyist, away from his Town Car, than a distinguished corporate keynote speaker in his dark blue blazer, maroon and blue striped tie and gray slacks. There was just a hint of silver in his black hair that framed a well-tanned face. He took only a few steps onto the stage, bowed and waved at his audience with a hand that seemed to be holding several large file cards and following a dramatic pause of thirty seconds or so, he turned and continued toward the lectern. After only another step or two he suddenly lost his footing on the hardwood floor and fell facedown on the stage with a loud crash while his file cards seemed to fly in every direction accompanied by several gasps from the audience. He rolled over, seemingly in pain, staggered awkwardly to his feet and proceeded to pick up the scattered cards as he hurriedly brushed himself off, all the while casting embarrassed glances at those in the front rows, who all seemed to be holding their breath in pained sympathy.

Finally he arrived at the lectern, placed both hands firmly on the poised microphone and just as he said, "Good afternoon, ladies and gentlemen," the cards flew out of his hand again. Now, with sheer panic and terror distorting his handsome face he raced around to the front of the lectern and began, once more, to pick up his scattered cards. He had only retrieved three or four, when loud and shrill female screams erupted simultaneously from several sections of the audience because, as he was in the process of leaning over and reaching for the cards, with his fanny to the audience, his pants slid slowly from beneath his jacket and fell to the floor, revealing bright turquoise lycra bike pants with yellow lettering proclaiming "Vote for Jo-Jo!"

Accompanied by both applause and cheers, Jo Jo Smith pulled up his pants, buckled and zipped them, then walked around the lectern grinning until he was facing his audience once again and said, "Gotcha! I sure did! Fellow speakers, hello! In my first year of public speaking, a long time ago it seems, I learned that before any audience will listen attentively, one must somehow get their attention and now, look at all of you . . . sitting up, watching and waiting for the next embarrassing or dumb stunt I might pull, aren't you? Well, that's okay because we're all partners in this special profession of ours even though we don't share the same ideas. You all know that old fable about the hen and the pig, don't you? The two of them were just gabbing and strolling down the road together, when they came to an old-fashioned diner displaying a bright sign that read HAM AND EGGS. The old hen stopped walking, nodded toward the sign and said, 'See, old buddy, you and I are partners.' 'The hell we are,' snorted the large pig. 'It's just a day's work for you but for me it's a real sacrifice!' "

Each of the speakers had a tiny high-fidelity microphone clipped to some part of their upper clothing so they could move away from the stationary lectern, if they wished, and still communicate with their audience. Jo Jo Smith took full advantage of his freedom and in the following fifteen minutes or so brilliantly imitated the voices, gestures and mannerisms of not only many of our better-known association speakers but others in the public eye from Richard Nixon to Bill Clinton, from Tony Bennett to Hammer, from Jimmy Stewart to Bart Simpson. Mary gave him a "7" and I nodded, having enjoyed him very much, although he wasn't the kind of speaker I was seeking.

The third contestant, according to his introduction, was Charles Ethan Gant, from St. Paul, Minnesota, representing Region Three. Unfortunately for Mr. Gant, there are days in all our lives when, no matter how professional and dynamic and impressive our past record and performances may be, it would have been better to have remained in bed. All of us, even the most powerful, have off days, and this was Mr. Gant's. He was a tall, handsome guy with a great smile and a smoothly shaven head which, Mary told me, detracted not one iota from his sex appeal, but he was obviously nervous and, even worse, was unable to hide it. More than once he seemed to search for his place as he shuffled his notes and what had commenced as a fine, strong voice seemed to lose its appealing timbre as the moments crawled slowly by. Every speaker in our audience, at least every authentic working professional, was able to relate, I'm certain, to this poor, unfortunate guy's situation and because they understood his predicament so well, it probably seemed even more painful to them than it would have been to a typical convention audience. At last, to everyone's relief, including Gant's, I'm certain, he finished his remarks, bowed once stiffly and hurried offstage. Instead of writing down a rating number on her program, this time Mary drew a question mark and turned toward me, eyebrows raised. I shrugged. Gant's Region Three included the Chicago area with scores of very fine speakers, most of which he must have defeated in the preliminary rounds, though he certainly didn't beat them with the kind of performance he delivered today. However, it happens to the best. I once saw Ted Williams strike out three times in a single game, years ago, when his Red Sox were playing the Yankees in the stadium.

As had been announced, there was a twenty-minute intermission following the third speaker. At least half the audience was now on its feet and filing toward the ballroom's doors. "If you've got to go to the men's room, hon, turn right when you get outside and you'll find the men's lounge down one level," Mary said. "I'll keep our seats."

"No, I'm fine. Gonna stay put."

"You look a little down, Bart. You okay?"

I nodded. "Yes, but it's beginning to look like a lost cause. Am I just getting harder to please with old age, or what? The first speaker, that blond ex-pilot. She was very good . . . damn good, but somehow, I don't know, hon, I want someone even better. Is it me?"

"No, because unless I've just been with you too many years, I happen to feel the same way. Nobody said this would be easy. If your old friend Napoleon Hill were here, he would say, 'We shall continue to persist until we succeed.' So let us persist . . .

and have faith. Don't forget that strange dream of mine and that voice promising that tomorrow would be the day. Well, this is tomorrow . . . and it's not over yet!"

The first speaker following the intermission was a tiny little guy introduced as Leo Samuels representing Region Two and he was from Jupiter, Florida. He was wearing a white, bulky wool sweater several sizes too large for him, and he pushed the heavy knitted material halfway up both arms before he tilted the microphone downward and smiled at us. My first impression was that he looked as if he would be more at home as an opening act at some comedy club than one of the six finalists in a contest to select the very best professional speaker in the world. I was wrong. The little guy was very good and he held our attention from his opening remarks when he said, "Ladies and gentlemen. Several years after the Second World War, Winston Churchill was speaking to a group of London business people who were seated in a room much smaller than this one. The person who introduced him smilingly made a good-natured reference to Churchill's well-known fondness for alcoholic beverages.

"He said, 'If all the spirits that Sir Winston has consumed were poured into this room, they'd reach up to about here'— and he drew an imaginary line on the wall with his hand, some six or seven feet from the floor. When Churchill reached the podium, he looked at the imaginary line and then raised his head up to the ceiling, sighing, 'Ah, so much to be done and so little time in which to do it!' "

Samuels smiled, nodded appreciatively at the loud laughter and said, "I, too, have so little time and so much to do. . . ."

The speech was excellent and delivered by a real professional who described many of the ways we waste time each day and how to correct those faults. Even his oversized sweater which seemed so much "out of uniform" to this old fuddy-dud had quickly blended right into our total impression of a charming guy giving a very good talk by the time he had finished, to long applause. I glanced over at Mary as she was printing "8" on the margin of her program. I nodded. Then, underneath the "8" she printed "but not for you." I nodded again, feeling more and more as if we were on a lost cause.

"Ladies and gentlemen," Dick Cobden said, waiting until the buzzing and chatter had ended, "our next contestant, representing Region Six, is from Blessings, Montana . . . yes, I said Blessings, Montana! How about a warm welcome for Patrick Donne!"

VIII

〜

Following Patrick Donne's introduction, our association president gestured hesitantly to his right before he turned, walked off the stage with a puzzled look on his face and stepped behind the curtain to his left.

Now the stage was empty. Where was Donne? Mary frowned and glanced in my direction, and I'm sure we both had the same concern as every other professional in the audience. Was there something wrong backstage, or was it just a little case of stage fright? Where was our fifth contestant?

And then, just as the murmurs in the audience began to swell in volume, a deep resonant voice echoed over the loudspeakers throughout the Regency Ballroom. . . .

"We are born for a higher destiny than that of earth. There is a realm where the rainbow never fades, where the stars will be spread out before us like islands that slumber on the ocean and where the beings that now pass before us like shadows will remain in our presence forever."

Patrick Donne was wearing a marvelously tailored glen plaid single-breasted suit, a white tab-collar dress shirt, an abstract jaquard print tie in several hues of blue, gray and tan and dark brown loafers. He was not smiling and he stroked his close-cut beard pensively for what seemed the longest time following his almost casual stroll to the lectern. Finally, in a very deep but hushed voice he said, "Those very special words you have just heard, written by an English novelist, Edward Bulwer-Lytton, before any of us were born, are perhaps as good a description as any ever provided mankind regarding what lies in store for us in that far-off place some call heaven."

I stole a quick glance at Mary. She was staring at Donne, and if she could feel my looking her way, she never acknowledged it. Now, for the first time in all the meetings I had attended at the convention, all I could hear was the audience breathing.

"Perhaps you are one of the many who have serious doubts that there is a higher destiny," Donne continued as he turned his head slowly to the right and then the left, "and that doubt is something only you can resolve with your God, if, indeed, you recognize a God. That, of course, is all up to you because faith is a lot like love—it can never be forced.

"Still, although only you can find your own way, after your life has ended, to that magic place where the rainbow never fades, I have an important message for you. One of the most difficult lessons we should learn in this life, and one that many of us never learn, is how to see and appreciate the beautiful, the divine, the heaven that lies about us right here on earth. Anyone . . . anyone . . . who has allowed himself or herself to be affected by events over which we often have no control, so that we despair of this precious life, is making a terrible mistake. Success, joy, wealth, love, fulfillment, are all available here . . . now! And yet many of us run for cover and hide, after fate has dealt us a bad hand, and from that moment on we live a life where tomorrow is as dark as tonight and instead of enjoying heaven on earth we wallow, unfulfilled, in our own private hell."

Donne stepped away from the lectern and raised both arms high above his head as that great basso-profundo voice reverberated throughout the room. "Those of you who have lost all faith in yourselves, in your potential, and in this tiny world which is the only one we have, please listen to me. I believe I have some suggestions that might help you change your life for the better. If you follow my suggestions and they don't work, you've really lost very little except some time and effort because you never believed your life could improve anyway, right? But . . . if I am correct, and from this day forward you could have followed just a few simple rules and altered the course of your life, taking you down a different path that might lead to gold and success, love and joy, peace of mind and contentment and perhaps, if you are truly fortunate, your own rainbow . . . if I am correct and you didn't bother to heed my words . . . my, my, won't you be sorry? So what have you got to lose? Are you with me?"

Amazingly, heads were nodding all around me. Professional speakers, all fully equipped with large egos of their own, rarely reacted to any speech in this way. Patrick Donne also nodded, turning his broad shoulders on us and walking very deliberately back to the lectern. Dead silence still prevailed. "Usually," he said, a slight frown appearing on his handsome face for the first time, "it takes me the better part of an hour to share some very simple suggested rules of living that, if followed, will change any life for the better. However, ladies and gentlemen," he continued, raising his right arm and glancing at his wristwatch, "even with the allowable extra two minutes I have only fourteen minutes remaining, but I'm still going to try to share with you, although in a somewhat condensed version, the actions you must take in order to enjoy a better life no matter how good you believe it is right now. Oh, and by the way," he said as he looked around, "I promise I won't get angry if you take some notes so that later you will be able to recall my—what shall we call them—suggestions for a more successful tomorrow."

Donne paused, clasped his hands together almost as if he were about to pray and said, "More than eighty years ago a great Canadian man of medicine, Sir William Osler, delivered a speech to the students of Yale University entitled 'A Way of Life.' Although Osler delivered scores of addresses and wrote many books in his lifetime, including a medical classic 'The Principles and Practices of Medicine,' Sir William may well be remembered for centuries to come because of his priceless advice to the youth of Yale. A copy of his original speech as well as his invaluable collection of books and manuscripts now have a home in Canada's great McGill University.

"Years prior to that Yale speech, Sir William was on an ocean liner. One day, while visiting with the ship's captain, a loud, piercing alarm sounded followed by strange grinding and crashing sounds below deck. 'Those are all our watertight compartments closing,' the captain explained. 'It's an important part of our safety drill. In case of real trouble, water leaking into any one compartment would not affect the rest of the ship. Even should we collide with an iceberg, as did the *Titanic*, water rushing in will fill only that particular ruptured compartment. The ship, however, will still remain afloat.'

"Osler, in his address at New Haven, remembered that unusual experience on the huge ship. He told the young people, 'Each one of you is certainly a much more marvelous organization than that great liner and bound on a far longer voyage. What I urge is that you learn to master your life by living each day in a day-tight compartment and this will certainly ensure your safety throughout your entire journey of life.'

"Osler continued, in words too powerful for me or anyone else to attempt to improve: 'Touch a button and hear, at every level of your life, the iron doors shutting out the Past—the dead yesterdays. Touch another and shut off, with a metal curtain, the Future—the unborn tomorrows. Then you are safe—safe for today!' "

Donne looked down as if he were grasping for the proper words. "Yesterday's failures and pains and heartbreaks are far too heavy a load for any of us to carry into the dawn of a new day. Leave them behind, all of them, and just walk away! And what of tomorrow? 'There is no tomorrow,' Sir William told his audience, 'the future is today!' Later he would write: 'Banish the future. Live only for the hour and its allotted work. Think not of the amount to be accomplished, the difficulties to be overcome, but set earnestly at the little task near your elbow, letting that be sufficient for the day; for surely our plain duty is not to see what lies dimly at a distance but to do what lies clearly at hand.'

"And so, my friends," Donne said, smiling for the first time, "my first suggestion you might wish to follow in order to achieve a higher destiny for yourself, right here on earth, is perhaps the toughest anyone ever made to you but, believe me, it truly works. Robert Louis Stevenson agreed with his contemporary, Dr. Osler, when the creator of his own *Treasure Island* wrote, 'Anyone can do his or her work, however tedious, for one day. Anyone can live sweetly, patiently, lovingly, purely, till the sun goes down. And that is all that life really means.'

"Let me repeat Osler's wise advice and my first suggestion to you. Live each day of your life in a day-tight compartment. This act alone will move you much closer to success and happiness.

"Another suggestion to assist you in achieving a better life here on earth is also from the past. It was without doubt the greatest secret of success ever willed to mankind, and it was delivered, almost two thousand years ago, by Jesus, in his Sermon on the Mount. In those powerful lectures to the huge crowd that had gathered, Jesus shared a great amount of wise advice with them. One of his rules of behavior, even after all these years, is probably not fully appreciated for the power contained in its words 'Whomsoever asks you to go with him one mile, go two!' Resolve right now, even as you are sitting here, that starting tomorrow morning you will devote more time and effort to please your clients . . . with no thought of extra remuneration or reward of any kind. Salespeople, you who normally end your day at five . . . continue until six so that you can devote more time to servicing your customers or perhaps even making a few more sales calls. Of course this type of activity, whether you are employed in an office or factory . . . no matter what your profession may be, actually . . . will not make you very popular with your peers because the name of the game, today, seems to be to do as little as possible for the check you receive. So be it. No one said you had to follow the herd. Just give a little more of yourself, in time and effort, in patience and caring, in helping and understanding. Do this tomorrow, and the next day, and the next, with no thought of any additional compensation. Try it for three months and then come to me, I dare you, and tell me your life has not changed for the better. Go the extra mile!

"Okay," said Donne, holding up two fingers. "I've now made two suggestions. Live each day of your life in a day-tight compartment and always go the extra mile, at home, at work, at play.

"Another suggestion. Never cut corners, never neglect the little things. Most of us break this simple rule many more times than we realize as we rush through each day, not realizing how much harm we are doing to our careers. Several years ago the great lyricist Oscar Hammerstein was being flown by a close friend on a sightseeing trip over New York Harbor in a tiny two-seater plane. When they eventually approached the Statue of Liberty, standing tall and proud more than three hundred feet above sea level, Oscar's friend banked the plane so that he could look directly down on Liberty's head, and what he saw amazed him. He remembered that this magnificent gift from the people of France had been erected in the harbor in 1886 and yet, as he looked down, he could see that every lock and braid of hair on the very top of the lady's head was as perfectly carved and polished as were all the fine details of her face and body and gown. But in 1886 there were no airplanes! Frédéric-Auguste Bartholdi, the statue's creator, could have saved months of tedious labor and costly expense by doing very little carving and polishing on the top of Liberty's head, reasoning that no one would ever see what had been omitted up there except possibly a few sea gulls and yet . . . and yet . . . every curl and braid is perfectly detailed and in place! There are no rough and unfinished areas! Never, never neglect the little things! Doing so can very often turn potential success into failure. Recently, an automaker, one of our big three, had to recall four thousand new and fairly expensive automobiles. Why? A tiny defective five-cent washer had been installed in the steering column!"

Patrick Donne paused, inhaled deeply, walked from behind the lectern toward the front of the stage, leaned forward and waved his right arm in a sweeping motion along the front row. "Well," he asked loudly, "are you all still with me?"

"Yes," they chorused, sounding like an exuberant first-grade class.

"Okay," he replied, now standing erect but remaining close to the stage front. "My next suggestion . . . never allow anyone to push your kill switch again. What's that . . . what's a 'kill switch,' you ask? Purchase an expensive automobile these days and you will probably also buy a burglar alarm . . . plus a little gadget called a kill switch. A few years ago those of us who had burglar alarms in our cars would merely step out of the car after we had parked it and turned off the ignition. Then, after double-checking to be sure the doors were all locked, we would insert a tiny key, probably in an opening in the fender, turn it and the alarm would then be set. If anyone tried to break into the auto, the air would be shattered with a loud, persistent scream, hopefully attracting enough attention to frighten the bad guy away. However, if the felon was bold enough not to be frightened off by the siren, after he was in the car he could still jump a couple of hot ignition wires in very little time, start the motor, and drive the car away, even as the alarm siren continued to wail. The kill switch changed all that for car thieves. Installed along with the burglar alarm, it is a simple-looking button wired to the ignition and hidden beneath the car's carpet in a place known only to the car's owner. Leaving the car, one would first push the kill switch button, make certain all doors were locked and finally turn on the burglar alarm. If a burglar broke into that automobile and the alarm was sounded, he could try till the cows come home and still never be able to jump any wires to start the car because the kill switch had completely cut off all power going to the starter. Oh, the lights would work, the windshield wipers would flap back and forth and the radio would even play, but the engine could not turn over and that car would not advance a single inch out of the parking lot!

"Now, I'm certain that only a very few of you here realize that all of us have a 'kill switch.' It gets pushed whenever someone puts us down or harshly criticizes our best efforts or makes fun of us . . . and, in one degree or another it's been happening to all of us since we were little kids. Ridicule, scorn, slights, insults—they all hurt and often their toll is so great that the little confidence we had managed to build up disappears until we finally stop trying to do better. How many parents, in moments of anger, pushed the kill switch of one of their kids by telling that little boy or girl that he or she will never amount to anything? How many kids then spend a lifetime working very hard to make their parent's prophecy come true?"

Donne paused again and tilted his head slightly. "Did I hit a nerve? Good! Just don't let it happen to you anymore. Don't push any more kill switches when you are with your kids and never, never let anyone push your kill switch either. Let me put it in perhaps a more familiar way to you. Never again give anyone permission to rain on your parade!

"Another suggestion. If you have been hiding behind 'busy work,' cut it out! It's something we all do now and then, but it can certainly put the brakes on a promising career and has, very often. You know the scenario very well. You are confronted with a real challenge, a project of some sort that is so large and important it might make a great change in your life if you handled it well. What do you say? 'Sorry, I'd really like to tackle that but right now I'm just too busy. Maybe later?' You're not too busy. You're just hiding . . . hiding behind piles of unimportant projects and papers and file folders that don't mean diddly in the larger scheme of things. Stop avoiding opportunity. Never hide behind 'busy work' again!

"Five suggestions. Note that I didn't say 'simple suggestions' because they certainly are not. There is enough power among them, when acted upon, to put a golden glow in your future. Live each day of your life in a day-tight compartment. Always go the extra mile, at home, at work, at play. Never neglect the little things. Never let anyone push your kill switch. Never hide behind busy work.

"If you follow those five, then the final rule of life I have for you will be easy. Never commit an act that you will have to look back on with tears and regret because you violated a law of God or man. Your most precious treasure is your self-respect. Guard it with all your strength. There is an anonymous poem which has been passed around for a few generations but it is still as wise and powerful as ever and I'd like it to be my gift to you as I take my leave. The poem is called 'The Face in the Glass.'

'When you get what you want in your struggle for self
'And the world makes you king for a day,
'Just go to a mirror and look at yourself
'And see what THAT face has to say.
'For it isn't your father or mother or spouse
'Whose judgment upon you must pass
'The person whose verdict counts most in your life
'Is the one staring back from the glass.
'Some people might think you're a straight-shooting chum
'And call you a great gal or guy
'But the face in the glass says you're only a bum
'If you can't look it straight in the eye.
'That's the one you must please, never mind all the rest
'That's the one with you clear to the end.
'And you know you have passed your most dangerous test
'If the face in the glass is your friend.
'You may fool the whole world down the pathway of years
'And get pats on your back as you pass,
'But your final reward will be heartache and tears
'If you've cheated the face in the glass.' "

Patrick Donne's voice had broken several times in the final few lines. He inhaled deeply and said, "I'm certain that all of you have probably gone on a long drive, sometime in your life, positive that you knew exactly the route to take to your destination. And then, after driving for a couple of hours or more, you suddenly realize that you are lost.

"You stop your car and open your glove compartment. But there's no road map there." Donne smiled. "The kids were playing with the maps, remember?

"Now you begin driving around, looking for a filling station, and you finally find one with a real friendly and helpful attendant. He opens his road map, shows you where you are . . . and then he shows your how simple it is for you to get back on course."

Donne turned his head slowly, sweeping the entire ballroom with his glance. "Well, for those of you who think you may have wandered off course a little bit in your journey through this tough life of ours, I hope that you will consider me just your friendly station attendant today . . . and when you get back on course, with your true destination ahead of you, if you happen to see a few broken branches along the way, please think of me. I left them there to mark your path to a higher destiny right here on earth. Have a good trip. I love you all!"

Everyone was on their feet, applauding, whistling and yelling. The ovation continued for more than five minutes, and somewhere during our constant clapping, Mary turned to me and held up both hands with all fingers and thumbs extended. Patrick Donne had scored a "10" with her and with me and with just about everyone else, it seemed.

I remember nothing about the final speaker, neither his name, his region nor the subject of his speech. I just sat politely in my chair, hearing nothing, trying to figure how best to approach the man from Blessings.

IX

When the telephone in our room rang, I picked up the receiver almost immediately since I had been sitting on one of the suite's three sofas with my hand on it. Jay sounded a little irritated.

"Bart, your damn line has been busy for over an hour. Is there trouble? Are you guys okay, or did the famous agent just take his phone off the hook so he wouldn't be disturbed by any nasty career climbers?"

"I'm sorry, old buddy. Been trying to locate Patrick Donne ever since Mary and I got back to this room. No one is answering his room phone and none of our people seem to know where he vanished to, not even our own president."

"Well, my friend," Jay chuckled, "I think I know where he'll be this evening, commencing around eight or so. You can bet all your treasury bonds that he's no early checkout. Mr. Donne will positively be attending our Night of Achievement dinner in order to pick up his check for a quarter of a million bucks as well as be crowned World Champion of the Lectern. A fine day's work, I'd say! Did you enjoy him? I mean, did he meet all your strict criteria, sir?"

"And then some . . . but where the hell can he be?"

"Beats me. Probably out celebrating somewhere. That's what I'd be doing. We'll catch up with him tonight, Bart, don't worry. I'll help. I want to be around when you reel this superstar in . . . if you do. Tell you what, I met a great member today, Sally Carver from Boston. Sally gives seminars on maintaining one's good health after fifty and she's got a figure that proves whatever she teaches must work. Anyway, I've invited Sally to go to the dinner with me and she accepted. How about the four of us getting together so we can dine at the same table, watch all the evening's festivities and then I'll help you corner Donne before the night fades away? What do you say?"

"I say it's an offer I can't refuse. Where shall we meet?"

"Well, you two are a few floors higher up than poor little me and, coincidentally, Sally is also on this floor. So why don't you two come by my room around eight and we'll all go down together?"

The staff of the Omni Shoreham had wrought still another miracle. As late as four o'clock in the afternoon, the Regency Ballroom had been filled with rows of folding chairs to accommodate every association member and spouse attending the contest to select the world champion. Now, only four hours after the contest had ended, the room held more than a hundred large round tables covered with red tablecloths, each table with fourteen place settings surrounding a giant vase of red roses. The ambiance of the huge room now seemed completely different from earlier in the day as the warm glow from glistening crystal chandeliers reflected off the golden-brown ceiling and shimmering stage curtain to form a perfect setting for the unique coronation that was about to take place.

The dinner was "black tie optional" and since Mary insisted that her attire for the evening was going to be a lovely evening gown she had purchased at Chermollie's in Manhattan nearly a year ago and never worn, I was duty bound to put on the white dinner jacket even though it felt a trifle tight.

Jay and his new friend were ready when we knocked on his door slightly after eight. Sally Carver was, indeed, a charming woman with not only a striking figure, as Jay had reported, but a lovely, almost wrinkle-free tan face forming a perfect setting for the largest blue eyes I believe I have ever seen. If the lady was only fifty, she was a miracle! Even as we were descending in the elevator, Mary and Sally had started chattering away. I glanced at Jay, nodded and winked. Like concerned parents, we both approved of his date.

Fortunately we found a table with four adjoining vacant seats not very far back from the stage. Neither Jay nor I knew any of the other speakers at the table, and so we went through the usual introduction routine all around. I missed several of the names because just as we started to introduce each other an orchestra of ten or so pieces, next to the stage, began playing an upbeat version of "We'll Meet Again." As soon as we had taken our seats, Mary tapped my arm and nodded toward the piano player, who was also directing the other musicians. "That's Peter Duchin," she shouted in my ear, "and he hasn't gotten a day older. Last time we saw him was at a wedding at the New York Hilton, five years or so ago, but I can't remember, for the life of me, who was getting married."

Jay was on his feet again. "Bart, if anyone comes by taking an order for drinks, Sally will have a Bloody Mary and I'll have my usual. I'm going to take a little scouting tour around the place to see if we can locate our man."

Unfortunately the Regency Ballroom was so congested with tables that there was no space available for dancing to Duchin's fine music, and so the would-be dancers began taking out their frustration by clapping loudly as well as pounding their feet. All that expended energy combined with laughter and loud conversations as well as the music to raise the sound decibels in the room almost to the point of torture.

Jay returned to our table just as the salad was being served. When I looked up he just shook his head, took his seat, saw that there were no drinks on the table except goblets of ice water, rose, dropped his napkin on his seat and headed toward the open bar. He returned in just a few minutes with a tray and drinks.

"Jay," Mary squealed, "you are absolutely amazing! How could you possibly remember that I drink Black Russians?"

"When it comes to women's drinks, I'm a master," he gloated. "When I need to find my garden tools, forget it."

Fortunately, everyone at our table seemed to know how to laugh, joke and relax, and so we all acted more like a bunch of kids at a school party than respected professionals from the world of public speaking and their spouses. The excellent roast beef dinner followed by huge servings of baked Alaska was as good as convention food ever gets.

Following a drumroll and fanfare from the two orchestra

trumpets, President Cobden finally stepped out onstage, smiling and waving again as he approached the lectern.

"Are we having fun yet?" he yelled into the microphone.

"Yesssss!" roared seventeen hundred adults.

"Are we all glad we came?"

"Yesssss!"

Cobden stood almost motionless at the lectern, obviously relishing the moment. "This is a historic evening in the history of our association," he said slowly, "an evening when one of our own is about to be recognized as World Champion of the Lectern! The Rostrum Professionals of America have played a huge part in promoting the growth of our profession throughout the world during the past several decades. However, as we continue to grow so that our membership now numbers in the thousands, we must never forget that small handful of visionaries who made all this possible, who had the courage and persistence and the burning desire to forge our organization out of little more than a dream. We are honored and so very proud to have had one of the six original founders with us throughout this convention. Ladies and gentlemen, will you all rise and join me in saluting the legendary Bart Manning!"

Reluctantly, very reluctantly, I finally rose to my feet as the applause and cheering grew in volume. Waving my arms and forcing a smile, I turned slowly in a full circle and then, feeling a little silly, sat back down as the chorus of sounds subsided.

Mary leaned toward me. "That was a first."

I nodded. "And, I hope, a last."

Next on the program was the presentation of the parchment scroll to those fortunate ten selected as new Masters of the Lectern. I had heard talk that there had been a special emergency meeting called with the board of directors earlier in the day to protest the masculinity of the award's title. This had become an annual and unscheduled element of each convention for the past ten years or so, but once again, I was told, "Mistress of the Lectern" had been rejected as the designation for those women fortunate enough to be honored with a scroll.

Of course, before the ten new "Masters" could be announced, all those who had been awarded the designation in past years had to stand as their names were called, bowing, smiling and enjoying another brief moment in the limelight. By the time Cobden had read his entire list, at least a hundred members were on their feet and looking down on the rest of us.

At long last, the ten new honorees, as their names were called, wended their way through the maze of tables up to the stage where the parchment scrolls were presented and each gave a brief acceptance speech. I knew none of them, but all ten seemed to be very popular choices with the entire crowd, and judging by their professionalism on the platform they probably all deserved the award.

When the final parchment recipient had returned to her seat, the ballroom lights began to dim gradually as the Duchin orchestra played "The Impossible Dream." Several spotlight beams drifted slowly across the curtain and stage until they all merged at the lectern as the ballroom continued to grow darker while two television cameras were moved closer to the stage on their tripods. The ballroom, after the music had ended, suddenly grew very still as Dick Cobden, holding hands with both, led an elderly couple up the steps to the right of the stage and then over to the lectern.

"Ladies and gentlemen," Cobden announced solemnly, "we

are now fast approaching that special moment that I'm sure you have all been waiting for. First, however, please say hello to Ted and Margaret Lee, who just happen to own the largest frozen dinner packaging empire in the entire world."

Both Ted and Margaret were obviously not accustomed to facing huge audiences despite their long status as respected leaders in the food industry. They both bowed very timidly to the applause as they nodded their heads and tried to smile.

"All of you, I'm certain," Cobden continued, "are familiar with Ted and Margaret's famous slogan, 'Our taste speaks for itself.' Well, very soon now, in a series of television commercials to be aired nationally, the World Champion of the Lectern, who is about to be selected from our own organization, will also be speaking for Ted and Margaret's fine foods.

"Through a series of regional contests," Cobden continued, "conducted during the past several months, the best speaker was selected from each area and these top professionals competed in a special program this afternoon which most of you attended. A special board of judges, all selected by Ted and Margaret's marketing people, then met in closed session and selected one speaker as the winner. That very talented individual, that spellbinder, is about to receive three very special prizes. First, he or she will be acclaimed as the World Champion of the Lectern, a title held by no other speaker in the world. Second," he said as he leaned down behind the lectern and raised a huge glass trophy, shaped as a lectern, high above his head, "he or she will receive this marvelous piece of Waterford crystal designed and created especially for this rare occasion. And finally, last but far from least, Ted and Margaret will present the winner with a check for a quarter of a million dollars!"

As if on cue, Ted Lee reached inside his white jacket, removed a yellow envelope and waved it high over his head as both television cameras edged ever closer to the stage.

"Ladies and gentlemen," Cobden shouted, "we have finally arrived at that magic moment!"

This time the two trumpeters in Duchin's band stood and the long fanfare from their horns echoed and re-echoed through the semidark ballroom. "I am most proud to announce that the World Champion of the Lectern . . . from Blessings, Montana . . . is Patrick Donne!"

Everyone in the ballroom was now standing and applauding. One of the spotlight beams moved slowly away from the lectern, across the stage to the right, past an area of gold curtain, until it came to rest on two wide brown doors with a red exit sign above. As if on cue, two waiters each pushed on one of the doors until they both opened wide, allowing Patrick Donne to enter the ballroom, waving and smiling. The audience remained standing and applauding long after Donne had joined the others at the lectern.

Finally, Cobden lifted the crystal trophy from the top of the lectern and placed it gently in Donne's arms, saying, "Pat, every member of the Rostrum Professionals of America salutes you. All of us envy you, also. What a great honor . . . and you truly deserve it, sir. You were absolutely mesmerizing this afternoon!"

Applause broke out again throughout the room. Donne murmured a faint thank-you as he bowed his head.

"And now," Cobden continued, "we have two very famous

people here who would like to meet you. This is Ted and Margaret Lee and they have a special presentation to make."

Ted Lee moved closer to the microphone, glancing around nervously as he waited for the applause to end. "Mr. Donne," he said hoarsely, "my wife and I are both honored just to be on the same stage with you. You are truly a credit to your wonderful profession and we are certain that you will be a great messenger for us in spreading the news about our fine products. And so, with no further ado, Margaret and I would like to present you with your other prize as world champion . . . a certified check made out to you in the amount of a quarter of a million dollars!"

Patrick Donne shook his handsome head several times, as if in disbelief mixed with awe, after he was handed the envelope. Ted Lee grasped his hand and Margaret stepped forward to give him a warm embrace and a kiss on the cheek. Then Dick Cobden lifted the heavy crystal trophy from the top of the lectern, gestured toward the microphone, patted Donne on the shoulder and to our cheers, whistles and applause led Ted and Margaret off the stage and down to their nearby table with its small white pedestal sign marked #1.

Donne, still silent, stood very erect at the lectern, staring down at the envelope that Ted Lee had handed him. Finally, but very slowly and deliberately, he tore open the envelope and removed the check. He stared at it for several minutes, so long that some of us were becoming uncomfortable before he finally looked up and said, very softly, "Friends and fellow members, I am very touched by the great honor you have bestowed on me today. And Ted and Margaret, I thank you from the bottom of my heart for this lavish award. I daresay that most people labor their entire lifetime and yet never even come close to amassing a quarter of a million dollars . . . in one pile. And yet, Ted and Margaret, I cannot accept this check. . . ."

Reaction from the audience was instantaneous. There were gasps, shrieks, moans as well as several voices shouting "what?" "why?" "huh?"

I quickly turned and glanced toward the front row table where Ted and Margaret and our association officers were sitting. Margaret was holding both hands over her mouth, her eyes opened wide in disbelief, and Ted looked like everyone else in the ballroom, stunned, as if he couldn't believe what he had just heard.

Donne continued. "I cannot accept this check as it is made out, and so I beg the Lees to grant me a very special favor. A month or so ago it was my good fortune to visit the lovely city of Portland, Oregon, on a speaking engagement. Following my speech, an old and beloved friend of many years, knowing my compassion for all children, took me on a visit to the Dougy Center for Grieving Children. Here is a very special haven where children mourning the death of a loved one can share their fears and their experiences as they struggle through the agony of their terrible loss and begin the slow healing process. The Dougy Center is named after a brave little boy named Dougy Turno, who knew he was dying from an inoperable brain tumor, and yet his magnificent spirit and attitude about dealing with death influenced hundreds of lives before he passed on. All who met Dougy fell in love with him and were deeply touched by his message. As ill as he was, Dougy was always saying, 'I can go to hospitals and tell other kids not to be afraid to die!' Dougy died in early December 1981. He received his wish, 'a new life for Christmas.'

"The Dougy Center functions on the policy that all children from the age of three through the teen years can learn to cope with their loss if they are given the opportunity to express their feelings and feel supported by others. In only a few short years what began as one special lady's dream, Beverly Chappell, is now reaching out to grieving children in more than forty locations across our nation and Canada. All Dougy Centers, I learned during my visit to Portland, are nonsectarian and supported entirely through contributions. To continue and to multiply their priceless efforts of repairing the frightened minds and broken hearts of our little ones, they very much need our help.

"I came away from the Dougy Center, that day, touched as I had never been touched in my life, and so I made a resolution. I already knew, by then, that I was to be a finalist here, this week, and so that night when I prayed . . . yes, I pray every night . . . I promised God that if I were victorious in this competition I would donate my winnings, all of it, to the Dougy Center in Portland. However, if I take this check and cash it, as it is now made out in my name, I will probably have to pay at least a hundred thousand dollars of it in income taxes and that huge chunk would never get to the Dougy people. And so, Ted and Margaret, I do have a great favor to ask of you good people. I will perform the required number of television commercials for your company to the best of my ability, as the winner of the contest is contracted to do. However, I ask that you please destroy this check made out in my name and issue another, in the same amount, to the Dougy Center. That way the entire sum will be a charitable and nontaxable contribution and all of the quarter of a million dollars will go toward comforting and easing the pain of tomorrow's grieving children, and the next day's and the next. . . ."

Several people at the table with the Lees immediately began waving frantically at Donne while they pointed toward Ted and Margaret, who were both nodding their heads toward the lectern in the affirmative. A warm smile suddenly appeared on Patrick Donne's face as he said, very softly, "Thank you! Thank you both, for all the little ones whose lives will be changed for the better because of you. I have tried for many years to live the words of a very wise person that history is unable to positively identify. The words were first written or spoken by either Victor Hugo or George Eliot or possibly a Quaker missionary by the name of Grellet, but they have long been my life's premier rule. The words are: 'I shall pass through this world but once. Any good therefore that I can do, or any kindness that I can show to any human being, let me do it now. Let me not defer or neglect it, for I shall not pass this way again.' "

Donne looked around the room slowly before continuing. "Perhaps some of you might wish to join me in this mission. The Dougy Center, I know, would appreciate your contribution, both large and small. There are always so many tiny tears that need to be kissed away and so many tiny hearts that need to be mended every day. Sorrow never takes a holiday. These little people, unable to deal with their grief, must be taught that life is still precious and worthwhile and that they have our support, our love and especially our understanding as we

all pass, together, through this world. God bless you, everyone
. . . and that's from all the kids. . . ."

And with those words, the World Champion of the Lectern
walked swiftly off the stage . . . to the longest standing ovation
I have ever witnessed in my forty-year career.

X

A heavy rain had fallen all night on Manhattan, constantly punctuated by bright arrows of lightning flashes and deafening thunder. It was our second day home after the convention, and both Mary and I were still in our pajamas and slippers, lazily sharing the morning paper while we munched on our Thomas' English muffins on which Mary had applied, after toasting, generous spreadings of Smucker's sweet orange marmalade.

My mission at the Omni Shoreham had been a complete failure. After finding, in Patrick Donne, someone who possessed all the special qualities I was seeking in a speaker, I had lost him. When he had walked off the stage, following his dramatic acceptance speech, he passed through the same exit doors from which he had made his entrance and then, quite literally, had vanished. Even after Mary had grown weary and returned to our room, Jay and I continued our search for the man, not only throughout the hotel but in at least half a dozen hotel cocktail lounges within a mile or so of the Omni. No luck at all. In the morning, before we departed for home, I tried phoning his room once more but was informed by the operator that Mr. Donne had already checked out. Frustration. Anger. I wasn't accustomed to losing and I didn't even want to think about giving up my dream of getting back into the business I loved so much.

Just to rub a little salt in my wounds, the previous night the "CBS Evening News" had carried several minutes of Donne's convention speech and once again we heard that great voice saying "Sorrow never takes a holiday. These little people, unable to deal with their grief, must be taught that life is still precious and worthwhile and that they have our support, our love and especially our understanding as we all pass, together, through this world. . . ."

Dan Rather, to further emphasize Donne's touching words, remained silent and pensive for perhaps fifteen seconds before he looked directly at the camera and said, "With people like Patrick Donne around, I guess there is still hope for mankind!"

Jay had phoned later in the evening to tell me that Peter Jennings had also done a piece, praising the first World Champion of the Lectern for an amazing act of charity, on his "ABC World News Tonight." The final straw was to just read, on the bottom of the front page of that morning's *New York Times*, a three-column piece on the "angel of mercy" from Blessings, Montana, and the dramatic gift of his entire cash prize of a quarter million dollars to "a little-known but very worthwhile cause, the Dougy Center."

"More coffee, hon?"

I lowered my paper, nodded at Mary and forced a smile. She

had dealt with my moods for many years and since our return home had apparently decided that the best way to handle this one was to leave me alone, which she had done by losing herself in a pile of paperback romances.

"So what are your plans for the day?" she asked.

The phone rang before I could reply. Good thing. I had no plans for today . . . or any day. I walked over to the oak-paneled wall near the large window facing out on Park Avenue and lifted the receiver from its wall bracket. When I recognized the voice I almost dropped the damn thing.

"Mr. Manning?"

"Yes."

"Sir, this is Patrick Donne. Please forgive me for disturbing you. I'm in New York for a couple of days, meeting with Ted & Margaret's marketing people. Ever since I arrived I've been wondering how to get in touch with you since I was pretty certain your phone would be unlisted. Finally decided to wrestle with this ten-pound Manhattan white-page telephone directory anyway and, miracle of miracles, found your name! For at least twenty minutes now I've been trying to muster enough courage to call you. Sir, you have been almost constantly on my mind ever since the convention ended and I was wondering if the rumor that kept surfacing at the Omni had any merit. Are you really planning to come out of retirement and become an active agent once again?"

The look on my face must have alarmed Mary, because she jumped up from the table and was now standing by my side, her hand on my shoulder, looking both puzzled and worried. I tried to phrase my reply so that I not only responded to Patrick Donne but also relieved Mary's concern.

"The rumor is absolutely correct, Pat. After a year or so of sitting on my duff and being pampered by my lovely wife and cruise ship stewards, I decided that kind of life was not for me. I'm too damn young to just sit around and do so little that the highlight of my day is a jog in the park. I attended the convention hoping that I might discover a good motivational speaker or two to represent since my old stable of professionals are either dead of retired. I did find one. You! I even spent several hours after the contest trying to make contact with you . . . in vain!"

"You did? God, I'm sorry, sir, very sorry. I had no idea. Hope it's not too late. I would like very much to meet with you."

"Where are you staying?"

"I'm at the Plaza."

"Nice place. How about today? Any free time?"

"All of it is . . . until three."

Our kitchen clock read slightly after nine. "Okay, tell you what, meet me at my office at eleven, how's that?"

I gave him the West 44th Street address and he asked softly, "Sir, is that the same office you have occupied for more than forty years, the one *Time* magazine called 'Manning's sanctuary in the heart of Babylon'?"

"It's the only one I've ever had and compared to most of the offices on Park and Madison and Lexington it's not much more than a broom closet. However, it's mine and I love it. Wouldn't be happy anywhere else."

"Well, sir, you may not believe this, but there have been many times in the past few years, before you announced your retirement and as I got more and more involved with public speaking, that I imagined myself visiting you there, always

96

wondering just what I would say to Bart Manning, and even more important, what advice Bart Manning would have for me."

"Well, let's find out. When you get there you'll find the old metal street-level door locked. Just ring the bell and I'll come on down and let you in."

"Mr. Manning?"

"Yes?"

"Thank you very, very much."

"You are more than welcome, champ! I'm certainly glad you called."

I had phoned Grace from the Omni on the morning that we were flying home, giving her the sorry news that I had failed in my talent hunt. I suggested that she just stay home for a few days until I decided what my next move was going to be, so I was alone when Patrick Donne rang our street-level bell. I dashed downstairs, unlocked the old door and let him in.

I'm not certain who was happier to see the other, but our handshake quickly turned into a warm hug before Patrick followed me up the narrow steps. He paused as I led him through Grace's small office, staring at our wall of pictures behind her desk.

Pointing, he said in a hushed voice, "That's Eric Champion, isn't it? I've got an old long-playing record of a speech he made to the National Safety Congress in Chicago back in the late sixties. He was so great!"

He pointed to another, smaller photograph. "General Goldfarb?"

"Yes, it is."

"I've read some of his speeches. Even on paper his words come alive. And I recognize that man, too," he exclaimed proudly. "Blandy. He played first base for the Boston Red Sox. Hall of Famer! You have certainly handled some great ones, Mr. Manning!"

"Yes, I did . . . and I miss them all. Come on into my office and please, no more 'Mr. Manning.' Call me Bart and I won't feel so ancient when I'm around you. How old are you, by the way?"

"I was thirty-two about a week ago."

"That's supposed to be a very fruitful and productive year in a man's life. Jesus did his most important works at age thirty-two."

Donne nodded and stared down at his hands. "But then they crucified him."

I didn't know what to say.

Donne leaned back in the old chair next to my desk and said, "How unusual, Bart. You're the second person in less than an hour to talk to me about Jesus."

"What do you mean?"

"Well, as you know, the Plaza is directly across from Central Park. After I had spoken to you I was just too wired to stay in that hotel room, so I took a long walk in the park. Shortly before ten-thirty I emerged from all that greenery, passed the statue of Bolívar, I think, and turned left toward Fifth Avenue, where I planned to catch a taxi to come down here. Suddenly this strange-looking street person began pointing directly at me, waving his old Bible and screaming hoarsely, 'You, you . . . this is your day! Life will change for you today! Remember the words of Jesus on the mountain, when he said, 'Ask and it shall be given; seek, and ye shall find; knock, and it shall be opened unto you.' He kept pointing at me and yelling, 'You, this is your day. Ask, seek, knock!' until I finally escaped into a cab on Fifth. Strange! Almost frightening to hear those particular words before coming to meet with you."

"Pat, are you a religious man?"

"Not really, I'm sorry to say. About once a month, on the average, I do attend Sunday services at a community church in Red Lodge, back home. I try to live by the Commandments but no . . . I'm not some kind of a religious nut, if that's what you're wondering."

"Tell me, was that street person screaming advice at you, on the corner of Central Park South and Fifth, in a wheelchair?"

Donne frowned and tilted his head sideways. "Yes, he was. You know this man?"

"No, but I had a similar encounter with him one morning while I was jogging home from the park a couple of months ago. Haven't seen him since, although I still take the same route home every day."

I didn't elaborate any further on my own curious confrontation. Instead, I said, "That was a great vanishing act you pulled after your powerful speech at the Omni. I had everyone but the FBI trying to find you."

He smiled. "I wish I had known. When I walked out those exit doors I went right down to the lobby and out the front door, where I jumped in a cab and asked to be driven to the Lincoln Memorial. Because of the time of night I'm sure the cabbie thought he had a real weirdo on board, and as I was paying him I told him to come back and pick me up at the very same spot in exactly two hours. Then I tipped him fifty. I managed to find a bench that was positioned so that I could sit and look directly at that marble masterpiece of Lincoln that was illuminated in such a manner that the stone seemed to glow. Before my long, solitary session on the bench, however, I walked up the long row of marble steps until the great man towered directly above me. On the inside left wall of the memorial, chiseled into the stone, is the Gettysburg Address, words that meant so much to me ever since I was in the first grade. Bart, way back then my beloved mother worked with me for days until I had memorized the words to that immortal speech. Then, on Lincoln's birthday that year, my mother encouraged me to tell my first-grade teacher that I could recite Lincoln's Gettysburg Address and so, naturally, I was asked to perform in front of my class. They applauded. They actually applauded! Before the day had ended, Miss Wray had taken me around to every classroom in our grammar school and in each class, to my great surprise, the kids cheered and applauded, even the sixth graders. I guess that lit the flame and the dream. Anyway, as I was standing in the memorial, so very close to that huge statue, I turned toward the interior left wall, bathed in warm light. I just stood there, alone, remembering how proud my mom had been and I read the words aloud with tears running down my cheeks. Then I retreated down the stairs to the bench I had found and just sat there with all my memories, trying very hard to put everything that had happened to me in perspective."

"And did you?"

"I think so. Bart, I need you. I'd like to be a great speaker, a real spellbinder, and I need your help to make my dream come true. Will you be my agent?"

"I'd be very honored to represent you, Pat. From what I've seen and heard, your potential is unlimited. I believe we might do very well together and what pleases me most is that I also like you as a person, not just as a commodity I'd be selling. However, some of my terms are rather stiff and perhaps after you hear them you might not be so eager to have Bart Manning handling you."

"For example . . . ?"

"My commission is twenty-five percent of the speaking fee we charge the clients for your performance. The client booking you assumes all charges involving your transportation to and from airports, hotel bill and meals. However, you arrange your own flights and report the charge to us. We will bill the client, collect and remit the total amount to you. All your flights are first-class. If they won't pay for a round-trip first-class ticket, you don't go, okay?"

He just smiled and nodded.

"And what are you charging, these days, for your typical one-hour motivational speech?"

"Well, Bart, the amount is always negotiable, depending on the organization. Usually runs between one and three thousand."

"Patrick Donne, you are the world champion now and the fee is ten thousand . . . not negotiable."

He briefly closed his eyes. "God!" He sighed. Then he looked directly at me and asked, "Would you mind if I continued to do a few fund-raising charity affairs at no charge as I've always done?"

"No problem. Now, you must understand that when we sign our contract I'll be handling you exclusively. Of course, by the terms of the agreement, as you will see, each of us is free to dissolve the contract with thirty days' written notice, no reason necessary, but while it is in force I will book all your speeches. Oh, I might split my commission with another agency if they contact me regarding booking you for one of their clients, but other than that every booking will involve just you and me and the client. Okay?"

"I have no problem with that. When do we start?"

"That depends a lot on you. How many future speeches do you have booked as of today?"

"Six, I believe. And the last one is sometime in October of this year."

"Then that won't be so difficult. Now, by any chance do you have any of your press kits with you? Do you use one to promote yourself?"

"I do use a press kit, Bart, but they're all in Montana. I'll be back home in a couple of days though. . . ."

"Send me a dozen or so. I've got a very talented advertising and promotion group here in the city who do a much better job than what I once put out for my people. How about glossy photographs?"

"There's a good eight-by-ten in the press kit and it's rather recent, but if you and your people don't like it, we'll get more."

"Great. That very first time we met, at the bar in the Garden Court, it seems you were telling my friend Jay Bridges and me about a cattle ranch that you had owned and sold."

"I sold it to my foreman when the speeches began to multiply. Never really had enjoyed all the thousand and one chores of a ranch, and when my dad died I probably would have sold it then, but it had been my mother's home since their marriage and I just didn't have the heart to ask her to move. So I kept at it until I lost her, four years ago, and when the speeches began to increase in number and I had a chance to sell the spread, I did. Kept five acres and a tiny three-room cottage, a messy combination home and office. Did all my own mailings and paperwork and bookkeeping and enjoyed it from the beginning. Still do. But I'm sure ready to graduate into the 'big-time' with your help."

I grinned. "How about that plane of yours?"

"My Beechcraft? Flying was once my greatest passion, but I've grown rather weary of it. I'd probably sell the thing if I had the right offer. It's in a private hangar in a small airport just outside of Billings."

"Pat, there's something else I've got to ask as we get to know each other. You're a big, handsome guy, but I've heard no mention of any Mrs. Donne. What gives?"

"You really mean . . . am I gay?"

"No . . . no. I was just wondering . . ."

"Eleven years ago I was engaged to the most beautiful girl in Montana. I lost her."

"I'm so sorry. Forgive me."

"I lost her, but not the way you're thinking. She loved me but she also loved her church and I guess when decision time came, I didn't stand much of a chance competing against God. The girl I loved so much has been a nun, now, for a long time. We keep in touch. She's teaching third grade in a parochial school in San Francisco. We exchange Christmas and birthday gifts and lots of mail. I've just never found anyone I could love and cherish as much as I did Jean Foley, but I keep looking."

"Well, I'm sure a big, handsome guy like you doesn't have much of a problem getting dates."

He smiled shyly and shook his head. "Someday, I'll find that special lady."

I handed him a large file card. "Print your address and phone number on this and when the contract is drawn up, Grace will mail it off to you. In the meantime, as soon as we receive your press kit we'll go to work on a new one featuring the fact that you are now the official World Champion of the Lectern. We'll do live mailings to all my old friends, the meeting planners and should be rolling before you know it. Also, when you get home, send me the exact dates of your six scheduled speeches and their location. If we get lucky and have the opportunity, we'll book you around them. Oh, and one more thing . . . I'm pretty certain we could place you on a few national talk shows considering you've already been praised by Rather, Jennings and *The New York Times*. Any objection to flying back here once or twice if we're able to spot you on a few in the next month or two? Might generate some action and make my job easier."

"You book 'em . . . I'll do 'em. I don't know how long Blessings will continue to be my home base anyway. I've been in love with this city for a long time, despite all its problems and my being a country boy, so I might surprise you somewhere along the line and tell you I'm going to become a New Yorker."

"Great! It would make my job a lot easier, especially in promoting you as the best of the best to all the national media here. If I can help you in any way along that line, just give me a yell."

The young man rose, extended his hand and said, "Thank you for a great opportunity. I've dreamed of this for a long time. You won't be sorry, I promise you. I'll give you all I've got."

"Pat, I have no doubt of that. You were my only choice. I'm not sure you even realize what a powerful force for good you can be in this country and this very strange time in our history, when everyone seems frightened and worried as they struggle to keep from drowning in a sea of misery, fear, uncertainty and chaos. The world seems to be going to hell, Pat. They need to hear your voice, your words, your inspiration. I'll be in touch . . . soon."

Donne glanced at his wristwatch. "Let's see, I've got an hour before I'm due for a meeting with Ted & Margaret's people. I think I'll do what I've been promising Jean I would do every time I came to New York City. I'm going to pay a visit to St. Patrick's Cathedral. Never been there, but this is the perfect time. I just want to thank God for bringing us together and I can't think of a better place to do it."

XI

🌿

One of the wisest decisions I ever made in my professional career was on that morning, back in the mid-1970s, when I finally came to the conclusion, with assistance from Mary, that I needed professional help if I was ever going to get all the benefit possible out of the press kits, brochures and mailing pieces I had been assembling and sending out to potential corporate clients for years. Even though Grace had always handled loads of my paperwork such as contracts and mailing lists, not to mention at least half my phone calls, I was still spending long days at my desk in order to keep my full stable of twelve professionals fully booked and happy. Somewhere along the way I had started to bring work home and, of course, the easiest things to transport were the many legal pads, pages of rough draft copy and artwork necessary to put together promotional pieces. One evening, working late on our dining room table laying out a brochure for our newest speaker, Gilbert Cobb, Mary had brought me a cup of my favorite herbal tea. As she placed it gently on my desk, she said, "Hon, you look like hell. You must be exhausted. Tell me, please, why are you wasting our precious evenings sweating over promotional copy, when there are perhaps five hundred advertising agencies within a few blocks of here who would probably be delighted to do all that for you . . . and quite possibly . . . if you will forgive me . . . do it even better? What are you, anyway, one of our country's best agents, or a writer of ad copy?"

And so, on the following morning at my office desk, I had opened the NYNEX Business to Business Yellow Pages to Advertising Agencies. Mary had been wrong. There were closer to a thousand advertising agencies within just a few blocks. Now, completely confused, I slowly turned the fifteen or so pages of agency listings until a small one-column-by-two-inch display ad in italic print caught my eye. *Dandelion Productions. The seeds we release produce for years. Two decades of proven experience and results in everything from direct mail to celebrity promotion. Call us. Terri and Vic Darnley.* 201 E. 50th St., 555-7849.

Just one meeting with Terri and Vic was all I needed to convince me that I wanted those two bright people on my team. It is impossible to calculate how much they increased the number of bookings I was able to obtain for my people because of the creative and appealing promotional material they produced. Their wise advice regarding my mailings as well as the national exposure they arranged, commencing with Eric Champion, on talk shows and network morning programs such as "The Today Show" was priceless. The secret to their success, I am positive, is that the Darnleys really cared. They made it a point to personally get to know each of my speakers so that when we met to discuss future promotion possibilities, as we usually tried to do every Friday, they could offer, as Vic had once put it, "custom-made" suggestions because they truly were familiar with the person we were trying to sell to clients.

When Patrick Donne's press kits arrived by overnight mail, I immediately phoned the Darnleys. Terri answered the phone, and when I very briefly told her the purpose of my call, her voice broke several times when she said, "Bart, that is the best news I've heard in years. We sort of suspected something was up when we heard that you two were going to the speakers convention. Are you really getting back in the business?"

"With the help of you two, I hope. When can we get to-gether and talk?"

"Well, tomorrow is Friday and Fridays have never been the same since you retired and our weekly meetings came to an end. How about ten tomorrow, here, like old times?"

"I'll be there!"

We spent the better part of Friday morning, after we had stopped reminiscing about our past triumphs and defeats, dis-cussing the various avenues we might pursue to best promote Patrick Donne. I could sense that Terry and Vic had almost immediately picked up on my enthusiasm and eventually we came to several decisions on how best to proceed. We agreed that I was to contact no old friends or meeting planners or pitch Patrick Donne in any way until the new press kits had been prepared and mailed. Also, the Darnleys insisted that we needed much more dramatic photographs of Patrick than the one he had been using in his kit.

I pointed impatiently at the pieces from Donne's press kit which were now scattered across the top of Vic's desk. "I hope all this won't take too long. We should have his contract in the mail to him in the next couple of days."

Vic smiled. "Bart, you're just getting antsy because you've been on such an extended vacation. Okay if we phone him today and ask him to come back to the big city for a couple of days for pictures and a meeting with us? I'd like the Matteo Studios on Lexington to do the shoot for us. We've used nobody but Matt in the past ten years or so for all your people as well as most of our other clients. He's a true artist. We'll tell your man to bring a couple of his best tailored suits along, if he has any."

I smiled. "Don't let the fact that he's from Montana fool you. He's got them. In fact, I'll even bet his blue jeans are tailored."

Terry shook her head in wonder. "Bart, I don't think I can remember when I've heard you so gung-ho on a speaker. You're not building this guy up in your own mind just because you want to get back in the business so badly, are you?"

"Positively not! If you could have been with me at the convention, you would understand. Until I saw and heard this man, everyone else onstage there, including several so-called top professionals, had all struck out on my score sheet."

Vic scowled at some of the press kit copy lying on his desk. "And when he does come, Bart, and the sooner the better, we'd also like to have a long meeting with him so that we can really get to know the man. His clients all seem to be small companies in the Northwest. Not much here to impress a Fortune 500 meeting planner, so we'll need to find a handle or two we can use. Okay?"

"Of course. And you might ask him to bring that striking

Waterford crystal trophy he was presented as World Champion of the Lectern. Could make for some dramatic photos. Also, in case I've forgotten to say it up to now, you two have an unlimited budget on this one. Do whatever you feel you need to do."

Terri waved her index finger at me. "You'll be sorry."

I waved my finger right back at her. "Never have been yet. Just remember to remind Donne that time is of the essence. The sooner he comes east, turns on his charm for the camera and meets with the two of you, the sooner you'll be able to put together his new press kit. Once we have all that, we can begin our mailings and, hopefully, I'll be able to get on the phone on follow-ups soon afterward."

Terri phoned our apartment that evening as Mary and I were watching the eleven o'clock news. She had made contact with Pat on her first try. "What a magnificent voice that man has, Bart," she exclaimed, "and I didn't have to do a bit of selling to convince him of the urgency of our project. All he said was that if Mr. Manning wanted him, he'd be here. He said he'd come to New York next Monday afternoon and be at our office at nine on Tuesday. Isn't that great? That will give me all of Monday to get in touch with Matt and arrange for Donne's photo session sometime Wednesday. On Tuesday he and Vic and I will have our long getting-to-know-you chat. Oh, and I hope you won't mind, I asked him if it was okay for you to be present and he said he'd love it. Also sends you his very best and wants you to know he can't wait to get started. I told him we'd remit the cost of his airline ticket and cab fares and that he had a room booked at The Peninsula, charged to your account, okay? So how did I do?"

"Does Vic know what a lucky man he is?"

"I doubt it. Remind him, will you please, the next time you two are talking."

I phoned a surprised Grace on Saturday and asked her if she would please come in on Monday so that we could finish as-sembling the full mailing list of corporate prospects that she had been diligently working on when I had called from the Omni with the sorry news that my scouting mission had failed at the convention and we had no speakers to promote. Then Pat's phone call had changed everything. On Monday we worked together for perhaps two hours before Grace patiently turned to me and said, "Bart, I can handle this, as I've always done in the past. Why don't you go on home and rest up. You'll need all your energy and then some when we get the new press kit and you begin phoning and pitching all your meeting-planner friends."

I purposely delayed my arrival at the Darnleys' office by thirty minutes on Tuesday so that Terri and Vic and Pat could get to know one another a little and talk freely without my presence impeding things. Apparently the strategy worked just fine. When I was shown into Dandelion Productions' small and cozy oak-paneled meeting room where I had spent so many productive hours with Terri and Vic through the years, they all had smiles on their faces.

After shaking Vic's and Pat's hand and kissing Terri on the cheek, I lied and said, "So sorry I'm late. My broker phoned this morning and said he needed my autograph on a few papers and it took longer than we planned. Pat, how's your room at The Peninsula?"

"The room is superb and the entire hotel is magnificent!

Plus I've already discovered their three-level spa at the top of the hotel. A tough way to live," he grinned.

I turned to Terri and Vic. "Well, you two, what do you think of this guy? Are we going to be able to sell him to the world?"

Dressed in a loose-fitting light linen blazer over a black T-shirt, Patrick Donne smiled and raised his broad shoulders defensively, waiting for the reply that came from Terri. "Yeah, I believe you might be able to get this big cowboy a gig now and then if you're not too fussy."

Vic said, "Seriously, Bart, from what Pat has just told us, it appears that Ted & Margaret's national commercials are going to do a great deal of the groundwork for us. Pat, tell him what they're planning for the initial one which they're going to be running nationally for at least a month."

Pat smiled sheepishly and shook his head. "As I understand it, the first commercial will open with a loud trumpet fanfare as the camera zooms in on the Parthenon followed by the same treatment of the Colosseum in Rome, then Philadelphia's Independence Hall and finally, the Lincoln Memorial as a baritone voice-over is saying, 'The world has known many orators in the past such as Demosthenes, Cicero, Patrick Henry and Lincoln.' Then Bart—and you are not going to believe this since you know where I disappeared to after winning the speaking contest in Washington—as the camera slowly zooms in on the Lincoln Memorial the voice will say, 'Our century, as it draws to a close, has finally produced a spellbinder of its own who is the equal of any who have come before.' As those words are being spoken I will step out from behind Lincoln's statue and slowly walk down the memorial steps, smiling and waving, while the voice says, 'Ladies and gentlemen, meet Patrick Donne, World Champion of the Lectern!' As the camera zooms in for a head-and-shoulders close-up, I will do a fifteen-second spot telling the viewers how proud I am to be speaking for Ted & Margaret's great dishes and I will suggest a specific dinner, yet to be selected by their marketing people. End of commercial as camera fades back and up until we are looking at an aerial shot of Washington. They told me I'll be doing my part at the memorial next Wednesday and they plan to debut the finished commercial on '60 Minutes' and 'Good Morning America' in four weeks."

Vic turned toward me, grinning, as he raised both hands high above his head. "Who could possibly ask for anything more? Tell me, Bart, have you guys decided what kind of a speaker's fee you are planning to charge for Pat's presentations?"

"Ten thousand. Firm."

"Not enough! Not when you consider what some of the so-called 'celebrity' speakers are charging these days. Of course, we haven't heard Pat do his thing yet, but—"

Donne interrupted. "Would you like to hear me speak?"

"We'd love it!"

"Well, a week from this Saturday I'm delivering the keynote address to the Nevada Association of Realtors following their annual awards dinner at Caesars Palace in Las Vegas. If you two come, I'll arrange for tickets."

Terri sighed. "It's been much too long since I've tussled with those lovely, shiny slot machines."

"Ten years at least," said Vic, sounding just as wistful. "And I wouldn't mind a few hours at the roulette table again. Terri, let's go! The work can wait. We'll fly to Vegas on Friday and stay for three or four days or until we go broke, and we won't even charge Bart for any part of the trip. Aren't we nice? We'll call our Nancy at Welcome Aboard and set it up tomorrow."

Terri excitedly jumped up, pushed back her chair until it fell over with a crash, hurried to where Pat was sitting, embraced him and planted a noisy kiss on his cheek. "Thank you, my new and special friend," she shrieked. "You have just performed a miracle! My husband is actually going to get out of this office for a few days with his wife and just have fun! Fun! Thank you . . . thank you!"

"Great," Pat replied. "I'll be flying to Las Vegas on Friday, after I do my Lincoln Memorial bit on Wednesday, so there'll be plenty of time for me to arrange to get tickets to you for the Saturday evening dinner. And speaking of dinner," he continued as he looked around at each of us, "would you all please honor me as my guests for dinner this evening at The Peninsula? I realize it's very short notice, but we need to break a little bread to commemorate this new alliance. Bart, of course that includes your wife, too. I can't wait to meet her. The hotel, as you probably all know, has a lovely restaurant, The Adrienne, and great food. How about eight-thirty tonight?"

The Adrienne's soft shades of salmon pink, glowing in the warm light from elegant sconces carefully positioned around the restaurant, served as an ideal setting for our celebratory dinner, and Patrick Donne, as I had expected, was the perfect host. After toasting each one of us with a few kind words, Pat paused and turned to me, still holding his champagne goblet on high. "Bart, we've been tossing that word 'spellbinder' around for the last few days, but I think that Mr. Longfellow, in his *Tales of a Wayside Inn*, described that person best. Now, I haven't recited poetry in public since grade school, but here goes . . .

'He ended, and a kind of spell
'Upon the silent listeners fell.
'His solemn manner and his words
'Had touched the deep, mysterious chords,
'That vibrate in each human breast alike.' "

It was truly a relaxed and wonderful evening, and well past midnight when Mary and I finally arrived home. As we were both undressing, I asked, "Well, hon, what do you think of the man?"

"Bart, he is as impressive and charming up close as he was onstage. There is a special magnetism, an aura of some sort surrounding him that's hard to explain. He's appealing and attractive and yet I caught myself lowering my voice a couple of times when I was answering his questions . . . as a child might do when speaking to an adult who represented authority. And with that handsome face and beard he reminds me of some of the figures in religious paintings in our church when I was little. He almost looks as if he should be wearing a halo."

"Mary, what are you saying?"

"Bart, I'm sorry, I'm not really sure what I'm saying."

Vic phoned our apartment on Wednesday evening to report that the photo session had been a great success. "Bart, he actually brought four tailor-made suits, four different shirts, a dozen silk ties and three pairs of Ferragamos with him. Matt was really impressed and I'm pretty sure we'll have plenty of

powerful shots to use. After Pat had said his farewells and returned to The Peninsula to check out, Matt told us that
Patrick Donne could probably make a very comfortable living
modeling clothes if he didn't make it as a speaker. Isn't that
something? In any event, Terri and I will begin to play around
with some promo ideas and we'll give you a call when we have
the pictures in hand. And, of course, we'll be watching the
man perform in person Saturday at Caesars. Then we'll really
go to work."

Mary and I stayed up on Saturday night, watching *Barbar-
ians at the Gate* on HBO until almost two on Sunday morning,
hoping that Terri or Vic would phone us from Vegas with
their review of Pat's performance. No such luck. We were
both having a late breakfast of pancakes and sausage when the
phone finally rang on Sunday. "Bart," said Vic, "Terri is on
the other line in the bedroom so that we can both chat with
you. Well, we saw our man . . ."

". . . and . . . and . . . tell me, for God's sake!" I exclaimed.

Then I heard Terri's soft voice. "Bart, he was absolutely fan-
tastic! I've never heard a better speaker, and that includes
your Eric Champion at his best! He had that crowd in the
palm of his hand from start to finish, and that's tough to do
with all the distractions in any of these Vegas hotels. That fee
you were planning on charging, ten thousand . . . ?"

"Yes."

"We both believe you should double it!"

"Twenty thousand? Are you guys crazy?"

"No, we think you should double it and then offer a guarantee that no one who has had the responsibility of planning a

convention or even a single business meeting has ever heard before."

"I'm listening . . ."

"Tell them all that if they hire Patrick Donne at twenty thou and they are not completely satisfied, you will refund all their money, including any expense charges you might have collected, providing they notify you within thirty days of the speech date. And we'll include a very special certificate of guarantee attesting to all that in your promotion package."

Slowly, after I had managed to collect my thoughts, I said, "There has never been anything like that before in the entire history of public speaking!"

"Bart," Terri replied, "there has never been a . . . a . . . spell-binder like Patrick Donne before!"

XII

‹❦›

Ten agonizingly long days later I was finally back in Dandelion Productions' meeting room reviewing the Patrick Donne
promotional material including a four-color brochure, cover
letter and even a six- by nine-inch envelope with no return
address, just my name in block letters in the upper left-hand
corner.

Terri and Vic sat across the table from me in silence, watching intently as I studied the fruits of their labor. Their four-
page brochure, probably the most important piece in any
mailing no matter what one is selling or promoting, was as
powerful a piece as any they had ever done for me. On its buff-
colored cover page, framed in silver, was a picture of the Waterford crystal trophy that Donne had received for winning
the championship contest at the convention. Above the
photo, in simple black Times Roman lettering, was the question "Why Not Hire the Best in the World?" Inside were two
striking photographs of Pat as well as simple copy, without a

trace of hype, describing the man and his accomplishments from managing a huge Montana cattle ranch to being praised by Dan Rather, Peter Jennings and *The New York Times* all in the same week—an amazing trifecta!

I finally looked across the table at my old friends and smiled. "You have really outdone yourselves. It's all excellent—the photos, the copy, the layouts!"

I picked up the cover letter that would accompany the brochure, ostensibly written by me to each meeting planner, which opened with a brief announcement that I was now back in the world of public speaking and would appreciate their consideration for any future bookings they might have. The letter then went on to ask the recipient if he or she would kindly take a few moments to review the enclosed piece on the World Champion of the Lectern whom I now had the great honor to represent.

"This final paragraph," I said admiringly, "is a marvelous touch . . . casually mentioning the money-back guarantee without even making any sort of a big deal out of it. Can't you just see most of the meeting planners reading this letter to the bottom and then doing this great double take as they back up and read that last paragraph again to confirm what they had just read? Love it! And this Certificate of Guarantee promising all the money back if the meeting executives are not pleased with Donne's work looks more authentic than most of my stock certificates."

"Bart," Vic said, sounding very relieved, "we've got ten or twelve other great photos of the man that we didn't need in the material. Take them along, and if you decide you'd like to use any of them in your correspondence with meeting planners, just let us know and we'll have Matt run off as many as you want."

"Thanks. Okay, let's roll on everything. How long before we'll have printed stuff ready to drop in the mail?"

"Barring any foul-ups, we should have the finished kits in your office a week from today. How many do you want to start with?"

"Grace is going to mail to our whole list, so let's roll with three thousand."

On the day after Labor Day I phoned Patrick Donne with the news that early in the day we had made our mail drop to more than twenty-seven hundred prospects and that I was sending him several copies of all the material that had been mailed.

"What's next?" he asked anxiously.

"Well, I'll allow sufficient time for everyone to have received and looked over our package and then begin making follow-up phone calls, first to my old friends who have booked speakers with me through the years and then I'll just work our way down the rest of the list, slowly and securely."

I could hear Donne chuckling. "How many old friends, Bart?"

"Oh, a couple of hundred, I guess. So what have you been up to since you left Manhattan?"

"I gave three speeches . . . in Salt Lake City, Boise and Portland. Two more and I'll be out of work, Bart. Just kidding. I'm so darn proud to have you representing me. Can't wait to start my career in the majors. As they say, it's nail-biting time. To keep from going bonkers while I wait, I've been riding my Harley, just about every good day, up and down Beartooth

Highway. I guess I've probably made half a dozen round trips from Billings all the way down to Yellowstone National Park. Nothing better than stopping that bike near a few special spots and spending a little time sitting by a glacial lake or walking along the tundra that is so quiet I sometimes feel I can hear God speaking to me."

"Pat, you never mentioned that you drove a motorcycle as well as fly a Beechcraft."

"Not to worry, Bart. I've never done anything foolish in either machine and I'm so safety conscious, I'm boring. I'll be okay. Just trying to keep occupied until you turn me loose. Never enjoyed just sitting around waiting for something to happen."

"Please be patient for just a little while longer, huh?"

"I will. Everything is under control, trust me. By the way, would you like an audiotape of my speech . . . a real good one? The people heading that company in Boise where I spoke are old friends of mine and so, as a favor to me, they brought in a crew and recorded my talk and I took a few hundred bucks off their fee. You might want to make copies and send them to prospects who can't seem to make up their mind whether to book me or not. I guess I was in high gear that evening because even I think this tape is excellent. Shall I send it to you?"

"I'd love to have it!"

"What I also have is the master tape which is on a large reel with all kinds of information on the cover that I don't understand but I'm sure you will."

"Great! With that we'll be able to make copies with excellent fidelity. Call me when you receive the material I've just sent you and let me know what you think, okay? I probably should have cleared all of it with you before we went ahead and printed it, but I didn't want to lose another week and I was pretty sure you'd like everything anyway."

"I'm sure I will. Did you say the mailing went out this morning?"

"By first class. All of it!"

"The timing couldn't be better, Bart. Most likely I will receive it before this weekend and then, on Sunday, Ted & Margaret's first commercial will air on '60 Minutes' and be repeated Monday, Wednesday and Friday on 'Good Morning America.' When were you planning to commence with our phone calls?"

"Next Monday. Talk about luck!"

"Go get 'em, boss!"

I didn't have to wait until Monday. On Friday morning after I had returned from my daily jog, showered and dressed, I was sipping coffee in the kitchen, when Grace phoned from the office, her voice sounding a shade more high pitched than usual. "Bart, Harold Titus just called. He said his secretary had just brought his morning mail, including our promotion package which was an answer to all his prayers. He would like you to phone him as soon as you can. Can you believe it?"

Harold Titus had been chief meeting planner for Latimer Investments, a chain of large brokerage houses across the country, for at least ten years, and he had often booked my speakers for their annual national conventions which were always held in the finest hotels on apparently unlimited budgets. I can never remember Harold quibbling with me about a speaker's fee. Through the years we had become warm friends, and since their corporate headquarters was based in nearby Newark, Mary and I had enjoyed many dinners with Harold and his wife, Arlene, over the years. I immediately dialed the number Grace had given me and soon after I asked for Harold Titus, I heard a familiar voice say "Harold Titus's office."

"Peggy, how are you?"

She immediately recognized my voice. "Mr. Manning, I'm so glad you called. How are you?"

"Just great, and how nice to hear your voice again. How's that old grouch you work for?"

"Hold on, sir, and I'll let you find out for yourself."

"Bart? Bart, is it really you? Thanks for getting back to me so quickly."

"How are you Harold . . . and your pretty lady?"

"We're fine. Mary?"

"Tough as ever. Harold, it's been much too long."

"I know, and I've never been able to accept the fact that you were no longer in the business. Then I received your great brochure on this man Donne this morning, and I don't know whether I was more overjoyed to see you had come back to work or to think that you might be the answer to a terrible problem I have. Your mailing couldn't have arrived at a better time. It was truly an answer to my desperate prayers as I believe I told your assistant in the office—Grace, is it?"

"Yes, it's Grace. She just phoned me. I'm still at home. Tell me, how can I help you, old buddy?"

"Well, first of all, my vanity insists that I inform you that this old meeting planner now has a title after his name. For almost a year now I have been Harold Titus, Vice President, Meetings and Conventions."

"What great news! It was long overdue, my friend."

"Bart, I find myself in a very difficult predicament, one that I don't believe I've ever had to deal with before. A week from this Sunday, on the eighteenth of September, Latimer Investments is having its annual four-day national convention at Trump Plaza in Atlantic City. We expect a record attendance of around fourteen hundred of our top people and perhaps eight hundred spouses according to the latest reservation figures I've seen. On Wednesday, the final night, our featured speaker was to have been Alex Shelley, who, as I'm sure you know, has written four or five blockbuster books on sales and motivation. His latest has been on the *Times* best-seller list of nonfiction for over a year now. Well, yesterday afternoon Mr. Shelley's Ferrari blew a tire and rolled over several times on Route Ninety-five near Daytona Beach and our world-famous author is now in a hospital bed with both legs and one arm dangling loosely in midair. Tell me, is your world champion's schedule such that he can come be our keynote speaker next Wednesday evening?"

Despite all my years in the business, I could feel my heart beating. Wow! I tried to sound very businesslike. "Harold, Pat Donne still has two speeches to fulfill that he booked himself, before I took over, and I'm not sure what those dates are from memory, but Grace has them at the office. I'll check and get right back to you."

"Wonderful!"

"Wouldn't you like to know his fee? As I'm sure you noticed, we didn't mention that in the mailing."

"I know . . . but I did read your money-back guarantee. Very clever. Okay, what's his fee?"

"Twenty thousand plus the usual—first-class round-trip ticket from his home in Montana and room and meals, of course."

"Will do."

There was no conflict with Pat's schedule. He immediately phoned his travel agent and then reported back to me that if he departed Billings early on Wednesday morning, he would be at the Atlantic City airport, on United Flight 368, a little after four in the afternoon, plenty of time to prepare for the convention's grand finale.

I told him to go ahead and book it and someone from Latimer Investments would meet him at the airport and take him to Trump Plaza. Then he surprised me by asking, "Bart, are you still jogging in Central Park every morning?"

"I sure am."

"Well, if I come into New York City on the morning after the speech, Thursday, and take care of some business with Ted & Margaret's marketing people, who are getting ready for us to shoot the second commercial, how about if I joined you for your jog through the park on Friday?"

"I'd love it."

"What time do you roll out of your apartment to start your morning runs?"

"I'm usually out the front door at just about six-thirty."

"Okay, on Friday morning I'll be waiting for you in my jogging suit just outside your Park Avenue front door."

"You've got a date, and about the speech . . ."

"Yes?"

"Break a leg!"

I immediately phoned Harold with the news that Patrick

Donne would, indeed, be his closing speaker on Wednesday evening at Trump Plaza and that he was to send someone to the Atlantic City airport to meet Pat at a little after four.

"You've just saved my butt, Mr. Manning."

"And you've just made my day, Mr. Titus!"

XIII

〽

Ted and Margaret's commercial on "60 Minutes," even though Pat had briefed me on its contents, was far more powerful than I had expected. Rare is the human being who would not appear small and insignificant standing next to the massive statue of Lincoln in the Lincoln Memorial, but when Patrick Donne stepped out from behind the white marble masterpiece by Daniel Chester French, nodding and waving, his powerful presence and warm smile, even on our television set, was compelling. When the commercial ended, Mary shook her head in wonder and sighed, "A star is born!"

On Monday morning I began phoning the names on my list of meeting planners with whom I had done business for so many years. Of course, each old friend had to be brought up-to-date on my activities, hear me explain why I had decided to jump back in the rat race and then we chatted about spouses and families and the condition of our health. Only after all those preliminaries were out of the way could I make my pitch for Pat, and throughout the day I heard repeated compliments on both our mailing brochure and Pat's dramatic appearance on that powerful commercial.

Corporate conventions are usually planned six to nine months ahead, so I was not in the least disappointed with the first day's results. My goal was merely to renew friendly contacts with those in a position to select big-name and celebrity speakers. The general reaction was that my old friends were happy that I was back and intrigued by Patrick Donne, most of them assuring me that they would certainly keep me in mind when planning commenced for their next convention, either regional or national. I followed the same routine on Tuesday, probably spending a total of six hours on the phone and renewing acquaintances with twenty-one meeting planners as well and learning that three of my old friends had passed on and two had retired.

At breakfast on Wednesday morning, Mary reached across the table and placed her hand on top of mine. "What's bothering you, hon? You seem to be a million miles away."

"I've been thinking that I should have gone down to Atlantic City to hear Pat do his thing tonight. After all, this is his first one for me and the very least I could have done is show up to give him a little moral support. It would have been nice. . . . "

"I don't think so, Bart. Patrick Donne doesn't need you hovering around and checking up on him. He's a big boy and your not showing up at Trump Plaza just confirms that you have complete faith in him. I really don't believe he'll be disappointed and I'm positive he won't let you down."

On Thursday morning I arrived at the office hoping that

Harold Titus would phone and report on Patrick Donne's performance as he had always done after booking one of my speakers in the past. Although I arrived earlier than usual, Grace was already at her desk and she greeted me with a smug smile. "Harold Titus hasn't changed a bit. He's already phoned. Shall I get him for you?"

I nodded and hurried into my office, picking up the phone on its first ring.

"Good morning, Bart."

"Harold, good morning. How did everything go?"

There was a long silence. After perhaps twenty seconds I asked, "Harold, are you still there?"

"I'm here, Bart."

"Something wrong? You sound strange."

"Well, my friend, I'm still trying to recover from last night. It was a closing session that no one who was there will ever forget, I guarantee it!"

By now all my inner alarm bells were ringing. Obviously something out of the ordinary had taken place at Trump Plaza last night, and Harold Titus apparently was still struggling to sort it out in his mind. I tried to sound casual but interested. "Tell me about it, Harold."

"Well, as you know, we were expecting a record crowd for this convention and we got it. The big ballroom had more than a hundred tables jammed into it for the awards dinner, which we always have on our closing night. The food was great and so was the music and entertainment, which we booked through the hotel people. They were a great help to us throughout the convention. After some dancing on a crowded floor, while the tables were being cleared, Robert Manson, our

vice president in charge of sales, went up onstage and announced the names of the leading producers for the first six
months of the year. Each was presented with a huge plaque,
and when they descended from the stage they walked over to
our table, where they received congratulatory handshakes and
hugs from our president, Horace Latimer."

"Sounds good," I said, still waiting for the ax to fall.

"Bart, table one, of course, is directly in front of center
stage. At that table sat Horace Latimer and his wife, Lucy, our
company treasurer and his wife, our vice president in charge of
sales and his wife, Sarah and me and . . . Patrick Donne.
When the ceremonies started, President Latimer and Lucy
turned their chairs around so that they were facing the stage.
After all the awards had finally been presented, one of my as-
sistants, Chuck Rosen, who had been a nightclub master of
ceremonies for years, approached the lectern and gave Mr.
Latimer a rousing introduction.

"As you know, Bart, Horace Latimer looks like a president
should look. He's tall, has great posture, chiseled features on a
tanned face and a full head of silver hair. When the entire
ballroom rose to honor our boss with a standing ovation, he
walked to the left side of the stage and up the steps slowly,
smiling and nodding at the crowd. At the lectern he patted
Chuck Rosen on the cheek, thanked him and proceeded to
speak to us for about fifteen minutes, telling us that he was
very proud of what we had accomplished during the first half
of the year despite a difficult economy and that he had complete confidence that we would do as well or better in the second half. Then he removed a folded sheet of paper from his
inside breast pocket and presented Patrick Donne, reading the

introduction perfectly, word for word, as you had requested. He waited for Donne to make the long trip to the lectern from table one, extended his hand and said, "Mr. Donne, I saw you in that commercial with your friend Mr. Lincoln. You both looked great!" And then, Bart, your man waited for the applause to end, still holding Latimer's hand, which he patted before he replied, "Thank you, sir. Knowing all that you have accomplished in your lifetime, I feel I am in the presence of greatness once again this evening!"

"That's my guy!"

"Of course, Bart, that produced another standing ovation and loud cheers. Donne waited calmly at the microphone until the audience had taken their seats again and Latimer had returned to his place at table one with his chair facing Donne and the stage."

I heard myself asking, "So how did the speech go, Harold?" Patience was never a virtue of mine.

"The speech was fabulous. Your man is as good as you said he was. The ballroom was soon very still, and that's always been my way of measuring whether a speaker is making it or not. Donne was powerful, dramatic, interesting, humorous and mesmerizing. Our people were truly spellbound. I remember that Latimer turned around in his seat, perhaps forty minutes into Donne's talk, nodded in my direction and raised his right thumb. Our president was obviously pleased and, of course, so was I. Then a terrible thing happened. . . . "

Now I held my breath.

"A frightening thing, Bart. Like everyone else in the ballroom, the people at our table were all concentrating on Donne and his message, and so the first inkling any of us had that something was wrong came from Donne himself. Like all good speakers, his head had been constantly turning from one side of the ballroom to the other, making eye contact with as many in our audience as he could, when he suddenly ceased talking in the middle of a sentence and leaned forward to stare down at Mr. Latimer, whose head had tilted backward as he clutched his chest with both hands. Before any of us could act, Donne leapt down from the front of the high stage, landing close to Mr. Latimer, whose eyes were now closed, his face covered with beads of perspiration as he moaned softly.

" 'My God,' I can remember his wife screaming, 'Horace is having a heart attack!'

" 'Someone call nine one one . . . get us an ambulance!' Donne roared as he knelt near Latimer, lifting him from his chair and laying him gently on the carpeted floor. Everyone was starting to crowd in, so the men at our table took it upon ourselves to keep them back. I watched Donne as he wiped off the old boy's face with a handkerchief and then began to stroke his forehead and cheeks as he said softly, and I believe I was the only one close enough to hear him, 'God, make him well, please. God, help him to breathe, please. God, help him to see, please. A sound heart is the life of the flesh.' He kept repeating the same words over and over as he placed the palms of both his hands on Latimer's cheeks and soon, so help me God, Bart, the boss's eyes slowly opened and his short, heavy breaths began to subside. It was an amazing thing to watch. Then Mr. Latimer tried to push himself up by his elbows, but Donne wouldn't allow it. The old boy just lay back on the carpet and I heard him say in a hoarse voice, 'I don't believe this was part of our scheduled program.'

"Well, Bart, the ambulance arrived rather swiftly and took Mr. Latimer away and everyone eventually filed out of the ballroom in a very shocked state. The few of us who had seen Patrick Donne in action, close up, didn't know what to say to the man except to extend our profound thanks. However, none of us quite understood what he did to bring our boss back from what appeared to be a one-way trip to the grave, although we all realized it was not the usual procedure for cardiopulmonary resuscitation. Those who had watched from nearby tables all went away telling each other they had witnessed a miracle and they were all asking, 'Who is this man?' "

"How is Mr. Latimer this morning? Have you heard, Harold?"

"I sure have, old buddy. He's out of intensive care and yelling like hell to be discharged. None of the hospital tests, including an EKG only an hour ago, give any indication that Horace Latimer had suffered any kind of seizure, heart attack or stroke last night. And yet, Bart, a few of us who were close by and have gone through the trauma of seeing someone struck down in the past will swear to you that the man had indeed suffered a heart attack. God knows he had most of the symptoms. He was clutching his chest. Pain! He had become very pale despite his tan, and there were beads of perspiration on his face. His breath was coming in short gasps and he had lapsed into unconsciousness before Donne laid him gently on the floor, wiped away his perspiration and began stroking his cheeks and forehead while he spoke to him. Bart, my mother dropped dead before my eyes when I was in my teens and she had all the same signs."

"Tell me again, what was Pat saying as he tended to Latimer?"

"As near as I can remember it was 'God, make him well,

please. God, help him to breathe, please. God, help him to see, please. A sound heart is the life of the flesh.' "

" 'A sound heart is the life of the flesh' sounds biblical, Harold."

"I'm afraid you can't prove it by me. All I know is that I thought we had lost our boss last night, but today he is still alive and well and I'm pretty certain that your man somehow saved his life. He's already checked out of the hotel, but when you see him please tell him that everyone who was in that ballroom last night will be forever grateful to him. And bless you, my friend. If you hadn't come out of retirement when you did, Horace Latimer would probably be dead this morning. God truly works in strange ways."

I continued to stare at the telephone after hanging up. There was a pain in the pit of my stomach.

XIV

Patrick Donne, looking very much like a Ralph Lauren ad in his black velour jogging suit and white Nikes, was leaning casually against the old red bricks of our apartment building on Friday morning, his arms loosely folded, when I stepped out onto the Park Avenue sidewalk for my morning jog at exactly 6:30 as promised.

"Good morning, boss," he called, flashing that handsome smile.

"Morning, Pat," I replied, extending a hand that he grasped firmly between his two huge palms. "Are you ready for a hasty round trip through the closest thing we New Yorkers have to heaven on earth?"

"Lead the way, sir," he replied, falling in beside me as I commenced a slow jog that I always maintained when coping with the usual wide variety of humanity found on Manhattan's sidewalks. Even at that early hour there were three occasions in the brief ten minutes it took to jog between my apartment building and Central Park when we were confronted by solitary old men in tattered clothes, crouching forlornly on the sidewalk and pleading loudly with passersby for money. Three times Patrick Donne stopped, removed cash from his wallet, placed it in the dirty hands of a grimy and disheveled panhandler who, in each instance, looked up gratefully at Pat and hoarsely said the same words—"Thank you, master."

As soon as we had crossed Fifth Avenue and entered the park with its lush greenery, our world immediately quieted down. Side by side we jogged along in silence, now at an accelerated pace, until we arrived at the Mall, that long, straight pathway lined with stately elm trees and busts of so many famous authors. Eventually we circled around the bandshell, went past the Bethesda Fountain and arrived at the Lake, a favorite spot for picnickers.

I could no longer control my curiosity. Slowing my gait, I pointed to a green wooden bench that faced the Lake and the park's only iron bridge, which had been made famous by decades of paintings, photographs and engravings.

"Let's sit for a few minutes. I've got to hear how the speech went."

Pat stopped jogging and smiled. "You mean your friend Titus hasn't reported to you on my performance yet?"

"Oh, he's reported all right. Gave you a rave review. Said you had that huge audience completely under your spell. I just wanted to hear all about it from the man himself."

Soon we were both seated with our legs extended to the stretch position on the newly mowed grass. "Well, Bart," Pat began, speaking slowly, as if he were considering each word, "I guess you would say that the speech was a success, but in that lovely hotel with its gorgeous ballroom one would really have to be a five-star dud not to be a winner on the platform. The room was perfect, the audience polite and receptive, and I gave them all I had. It being my first speech for you, I didn't dare let you down. On a scale of zero to ten, I guess I'd give myself a strong eight."

I nodded but remained silent, waiting for him to continue. Pat finally turned toward me and asked, "Did Mr. Titus tell you what happened toward the end of my talk?"

"He gave me some of the details. I figured I'd get the rest from you."

"Well," Pat sighed, "the speech had been going along pretty well and I was in the home stretch when I happened to look down at the head table, which was just in front of the lectern. Mr. Latimer had suddenly slumped backward in his chair as if he were having some sort of attack or stroke. I guess everyone was paying such close attention to me that I noticed he was having trouble before anyone else. I immediately stopped talking, ran around the lectern and jumped down off the stage to try to help the man if I could. I guess he was unconscious for a while, but he finally came to and was rushed off to the hospital. I phoned the hospital last night from my hotel here and they told me he was no longer in intensive care and was expected to be released sometime this weekend, so I guess it all turned out okay. However, I still like my ending to the speech better than his." He grinned sheepishly.

I leaned toward Pat and patted his shoulder. " 'A sound heart is the life of the flesh.' "

"What?"

" 'A sound heart is the life of the flesh.' Harold Titus, who was standing quite close to you when you were administering to Horace Latimer, said this was one of the phrases he believes he heard you repeating over the unconscious man. Some sort of prayer?"

Pat raised his head so that he was now staring over the water and trees toward the city's towering skyscrapers beyond. "Bart, those particular words are Solomon's from The Book of Proverbs. They are also part of a special prayer that I was taught when I was very young by an old Crow Indian who worked for years on our ranch. His name was Brightest Star and he was very kind to me when I was growing up. He taught me to appreciate the handiwork of God from the smallest worm or ant to the largest moose or pine tree. He taught me to have pity and patience and love for all living things, and that I should never allow a day to pass without doing good for someone, because I might never get the opportunity again. He also taught me how to say special words over anyone who was very sick and he assured me that God would positively hear me and consider my request."

"Have you used those special words before?"

He nodded. "They have never failed me."

"Are those the same words you repeated over Mr. Latimer?"

Patrick Donne nodded. Then he inhaled deeply, placed the palms of his hands gently against my cheeks and said, in that spine-tingling basso-profundo voice, "God, make him well, please. God, help him to breathe, please. God, help him to see, please, A sound heart is the life of the flesh."

He removed his hands and looked away. I started to say that it seemed to be a rather strange form of cardiopulmonary re-

suscitation, but I couldn't. Instead, I said, "An American Indian quoting Solomon. That's quite a twist."

"Why? We all share the same God. Someday the people on
this tiny ball of earth will stop cursing, hurting and killing one
another and realize that we're all from the same assembly line
no matter how different our fenders or wheels or paint jobs
are. We are truly all brothers and sisters. We all shed tears, we
all smile, we all feel pain, we all grow hungry. None of us
should lay our head on a pillow at night without planning to
reach out to another human being during the following day.
Even something as insignificant as a hug, if one has nothing
else to share, can be a precious gift."

A tiny sparrow suddenly swooped down from behind us,
landing only a few yards from our feet, pecking at what looked
like a discarded cookie.

"Bart, are you familiar with Oscar Wilde's great fable about
the happy prince?"

"No, I don't believe so."

"Seeing that little bird reminded me of it. It's one of my fa-
vorites on the subject of giving with no thought of any reward,
which I keep trying to sell the world. According to Wilde's
powerful classic, a very special and elegant statue of a happy
prince stood on a tall column high above a great city. The
prince's body was covered with thin leaves of fine gold, for
eyes he had huge sapphires and on his sword hilt there was a
large red ruby.

"One day, Bart, a little swallow who had delayed his winter
journey to Egypt much too long, paused on his hurried trip
south to put up for the night between the feet of the statue.
However, the swallow couldn't sleep because of the sound of

the prince weeping, so he flew up, landed on the prince's shoulder and asked him why he was crying.

"The prince replied that although everyone called him the happy prince, he was not happy at all. How could he possibly be happy, he asked the little bird, when from his station high above the city he could see so many people who needed help, food, care, love and tenderness. 'Will you please help me, little bird? Will you help me to give myself away?' The bird agreed.

"First, the swallow removed the ruby from the prince's sword and carried it down to a frightened young mother tending her sick child in a cold attic. Then the little bird flew all the way back to the prince, removed one sapphire eye and carried it down to an old man in a small shack who had not eaten for two days. Then he flew all the way back to the prince once more, removed the other sapphire eye and left it in the city at the feet of a little matchgirl. One by one, the swallow carefully removed all the leaves of gold from the prince's body and distributed them to the poor and helpless children of the city.

"And then the frigid blasts of winter struck, and since the prince's body was no longer protected, his leaden heart cracked. And, unable to protect himself from the cold, the tiny swallow also perished.

"One morning, God called his angels together and pointed down to the city, saying, 'Bring me the two most precious things from that place.' And when the angels returned they were carrying the cracked heart of the prince . . . and the body of a tiny dead bird. It's called 'love with no price tag,' my friend, and if we don't start learning how to live that way, our lives will all be worthless."

I nodded. "Thanks. That was very special. Those three panhandlers that we passed on the way here to the park . . . do you stop and give to all of them?"

He nodded, staring down at his hands. "Always. Every one of them is a work of God. There was a time in each of their lives when they had all the dreams and hopes and ambitions that you had, that I had. Teachers, parents and lovers cared for them, worked with them, planned with them. They had savings accounts, picked flowers, kept diaries, changed flat tires. They lived and laughed and could never have possibly imagined that one day they would be living in the gutter. They have hearts, Bart, and those hearts beat exactly like mine and yours."

"So you reach out to every one of them?"

"I do. I even bring that philosophy with me when I walk out onto the stage and face an audience. I'm really trying to do a sales job on each person in that crowd, trying to convince them to use the few simple but powerful principles that I share with them to build a better life so that they can fulfill their dreams without stumbling, again and again, until they also end up in a swamp of despair and fear. When I'm onstage, Bart, I give it my all, not for the fee I'm being paid . . . never . . . I'm working as hard as I do so that I can hopefully reach my audience and point out the way to a bright tomorrow for them. I don't know how many times I've looked out over the crowd, focused in on some well-dressed nice-looking guy or gal and pictured them standing on a corner somewhere, in dirty, tattered clothes, trying to sell pencils so that they could buy another bottle of cheap wine. Of course that's not what any of them, as they sit and listen to me, are planning for their future, but then, those panhandlers we saw this morning, when they were

143

each ten years old, never expected to be standing, someday, on a busy Manhattan street corner, begging."

"You are truly an amazing man, Patrick Donne. I'm proud I'm your friend."

He shook his head violently. "I'm not amazing at all, Bart. There are a few simple lines from one of Emily Dickinson's poems that pretty much guide my life. . . .

> 'If I can stop one heart from breaking,
> 'I shall not live in vain;
> 'If I can ease one life the aching,
> 'Or cool one pain,
> 'Or help one fainting robin
> 'Unto his nest again,
> 'I shall not live in vain.' "

Patrick Donne rose, walked a few paces from the bench, extended both his arms in a sweeping motion and said, "Bart, look around this beautiful place you call heaven on earth. What do you know of its past?"

"Not as much as I should, I'm afraid."

"Well, you will admit that there is now an army of homeless people on the sidewalks of Manhattan, correct?"

"And I'm afraid the number is growing. . . . "

"Did you know that in the middle of the last century the so-called street people all gathered here? What is now Central Park was a dismal and smelly swamp, and all the homeless, along with their animals, camped here until Washington Irving, William Cullen Bryant and a small, powerful contingent of men who truly loved this city sold the public on establishing a huge park here. The winning design, after a hard-fought competition, earned a prize of two thousand dollars—imagine—and then the homeless fought, some to their death, to keep their only home when the city finally acquired this huge square of land and began clearing it. A tremendous army of tough, unemployed Irish immigrants, after years and years of digging and draining and landscaping, eventually produced this beautiful refuge for all to share."

"Pat, I'm ashamed to say I knew very little of that."

"This lovely place has been a haven to the homeless more than once, Bart. During Herbert Hoover's last two years of office, Central Park became the only address for thousands of unemployed and their long rows of flimsy shacks were known as 'Hooverville.' "

"Pat, how the hell do you know so much about this place? Research on Central Park . . . or the homeless?"

He grinned. "Guess."

Instead of walking all the way to the reservoir, on the park's eastern border, we turned before we got to the Pond and headed back south, past the children's playground, Conservatory Pond, Hans Christian Andersen's statue and the Children's Zoo before emerging through Grand Army Plaza and heading for the corner of Central Park South and Fifth Avenue.

I heard that unforgettable screeching voice before I saw him, leaning forward in his wheelchair, waving his Bible high above his head as he tormented and harangued each passerby.

"Beware of false prophets!"

"No man can serve two masters!"

"Refuse the evil, and choose the good!"

From his tattered red T-shirt to his dingy sneakers, he was dressed exactly as he was on that fateful day when I had suddenly turned south to avoid confrontation with him. As we approached, he saw me, pointed directly at me and screamed, "You! You! It is better to trust in the Lord than to put confidence in man! Hear me! You! You . . . !"

Suddenly the raving vagrant stopped screaming. Now, mouth open, he was staring at Pat. We drew closer and closer to the wheelchair. The old boy dropped his Bible in his lap, raised his hands clasped in prayer and, looking directly up at Patrick Donne, he said softly as we passed, "Hallowed be thy name. . . ."

XV

After showering, shaving and dressing I joined Mary in the kitchen for my usual second cup of coffee before heading to the office. She was frowning at me until I finally asked, "What's wrong?"

"So where is he?"

"Patrick?"

She shook her head and sighed impatiently. "Yes, my husband, Patrick, Patrick Donne. Wasn't he joining you this morning for your jaunt through Central Park?"

"He did. We parted just a few minutes ago. I tried to lure him up here with promises that you would make a batch of your special blueberry pancakes for him, but he has a plane to catch for Florida at ten. They're shooting Pat's second commercial for Ted & Margaret's Frozen Dinners at the base of a launching pad at Cape Canaveral, can you believe?"

"And it's okay with our government?"

"I guess. Most of the country is still talking about Patrick's first spot from the Lincoln Memorial. He said that the reception was so great that Ted & Margaret's have decided to run each of the final eight commercials for four consecutive weeks on '60 Minutes' as well as three times a week on 'Good Morning, America.' Talk about fabulous exposure. If the other commercials turn out to be as powerful as his first, I'll be getting more requests for speeches than he could ever possibly handle."

Mary laughed, kissed me on the cheek and said, "Poor baby. Oh, I almost forgot. Call Jay Bridges. He's at home. The number is on the pad hanging next to the kitchen phone."

"Something wrong?"

"I don't think so. The old boy sounded real upbeat. Asked me if I would please have my genius of a husband honor him with a call whenever it was convenient . . . if you can make any sense out of that."

I went to the phone and punched out the number Mary had scribbled on our message pad. Jay Bridges's familiar voice said, "Good morning. It's another lovely day here in Memphis."

"And it's not too shabby here in Manhattan either."

"Bart, you old fox, I've been tipping my hat to you for many years, but this latest stunt of yours calls for at least a touching of my knee to the floor in reverence. You certainly haven't lost your touch, that's for certain."

"Jay, what the hell are you talking about?"

"Oh, sure, this is all a surprise to you. I'm talking about that fascinating piece on your man, Patrick Donne, which happens to be on the first page of the Life section of today's *USA Today.*"

"We don't take *USA Today*, so I have not seen whatever

you are talking about and I don't know anything about it. Do you have it handy?"

"I'm holding it, Bart. When the phone rang I figured it was you."

"Would you mind reading it to me . . . please?"

"It's a single-column piece, five paragraphs long, and considering that the subject of the piece is about the possible saving of a life, we have this amazing coincidence of it appearing right next to the Lifeline column . . . Lifeline, Bart, which always runs down the entire left-hand side of the first page of the Life section. The article has a bold heading which reads 'Does this spellbinder also perform miracles?'"

"Oh, God," I heard myself moaning.

Jay noisily cleared his throat twice and commenced reading. "'Tall, handsome and with a commanding voice, Patrick Donne is one of that rare and rather exclusive group of professionals known as motivational and inspirational speakers. Is your company having its annual convention? If so, they could probably use a dynamic individual like Donne, after three days of dull business meetings, to send everyone back to their hometown on a high and positive note, prepared to set new sales records as they tackle the world again with renewed vigor.

"'Few in the business of public speaking would question that Patrick Donne, ex-cowboy from Montana, is one of the best motivational speakers in the nation. Back in July, at the annual convention of Rostrum Professionals of America, an organization with thousands of members, Donne was victorious in a speakers contest against most of the top professionals in the business and was crowned World Champion of the Lectern.

" 'Donne's victory, however, was worth far more than a Waterford crystal trophy. The founders of Ted & Margaret's Frozen Dinners, sponsors of the oratorical "shoot-out," also presented the winner with a check for a quarter of a million dollars, an advance payment for his appearance in a series of nine television commercials "speaking" about their products. Donne shocked the huge crowd by returning the check as soon as it was presented to him, asking that another be issued, instead, in the full amount, to the Dougy Center, headquartered in Portland, Oregon, a nonprofit organization devoted to teaching youth how to better deal with the loss of a loved one. His touching and unselfish gesture attracted national attention at the time.

" 'Once again Patrick Donne is in the news. Last Wednesday evening he was delivering his powerful keynote address during the final evening of a convention of nationwide Latimer Investments representatives and their spouses at the Trump Plaza in Atlantic City. Toward the conclusion of his talk, according to some of those present, Donne suddenly ceased speaking, raced to the edge of the podium and leapt down into the audience, landing close to the table where company president, Horace Latimer, had suddenly slumped backward in his chair, clutching his chest and moaning. Latimer was obviously having an attack of some sort.

" 'In the confusion, no one is quite certain what followed except that Donne apparently lifted the stricken man from his chair and placed him gently on the carpeted floor. Then, according to one witness, he began to stroke Latimer's perspiring face as he spoke to the suffering man so softly that no one was able to hear his words. Soon Latimer had regained consciousness and was sitting up, even managing a faint smile at Donne before the ambulance arrived. Latimer spent the remainder of the night in intensive care but several physicians consulted all reported that there was no sign of any coronary damage and he has been released. Neither Patrick Donne nor his agent could be reached for comment, but there are many Latimer Investments employees who are quite certain that they were witnesses to a miracle, a true modern-day "laying on of hands." ' "

Fifteen minutes or more later, when Jay and I ended our telephone conversation, I still had not convinced him that I was not involved in any way with the USA Today piece. Most interesting, I thought, was that not once during our discussion did Jay ever ask me what Patrick had told me about the incident or whether I personally believed a miracle of any sort had taken place.

To help myself think clearly and rationally, I walked to my office, that morning, and by the time I arrived on West 44th Street I had decided to get some expert advice on how best to handle the situation before it got out of hand. I just didn't want the public at large, and especially prospective clients, to start thinking of Patrick Donne as anything but the magnificent speaker that he was. I phoned the Darnleys. Vic was out on business but Terri listened patiently until I had covered most of the details before she said, "Bart, Vic and I have seen the piece and already had a little chat about it. It upsets us too, primarily because it was projecting the wrong image of Pat, but we decided to say nothing unless you called and asked our opinion. Our opinion is that you should ignore the matter or, at the very least, treat it lightly. Vic and I were even making up questions that either of you might be asked about the affair by the media or potential clients and most of the answers we could come up with would only further confuse the matter. The most that should be done, if either you or Pat find yourself confronted with questions you cannot possibly avoid, is to just say that he only performed a little first aid just as any other human would have done under similar circumstances and let it go at that. However, our bottom-line advice for both you and Pat is to say as little as possible about the affair, volunteer no information and let time gradually erase the matter from everyone's memory. In a week or so it should have all faded away."

The Darnleys' advice, wise though it seemed, was not easy to follow. For several days after the article's appearance, almost every phone call I made to meeting planners, as I continued to follow up on my mailing, produced a question or two about Patrick's "miracle in Atlantic City" but gradually, as Terri had predicted, the entire matter seemed to have been forgotten.

Never before, not even at the height of Eric Champion's popularity, did I enjoy the success that followed in booking Patrick. Ted & Margaret's powerful and very memorable commercials, each presenting Patrick Donne as the World Champion of the Lectern, shown to the nation week after week, soon made him almost as recognizable to the average American as our president or Michael Jackson or Peanuts. Following his Cape Canaveral appearance, he delivered his Ted & Margaret's commercials while leaning against a goal post in the Rose Bowl, rounding a tight turn at the Indianapolis Motor Speedway in an Indy car, building a small campfire on a red ridge of rock over a breathtaking portion of the Grand

Canyon, strolling across the Golden Gate Bridge, softly strumming a guitar as he sat on the lush grass outside of Graceland, patting the Liberty Bell and rowing a small canoe on the still waters of Thoreau's Walden Pond.

The first four weeks of my contacting meeting planners had produced three future speaker engagement contracts, each at $20,000 plus expenses. In the following month Grace mailed out seven more contracts and then twelve during the third month. My problem then became one that all agents wish they had. Actually I had two problems. First, it became necessary for me to stay in constant contact with the promotion and publicity people at Ted & Margaret's so that I could coordinate Pat's scheduled speeches with the company's commercial shootings at the various locations. Secondly, as I continued to build on Pat's schedule, I had to find out from the man himself just how many bookings he felt he could handle each month without fatigue setting in and marring his performance. The speeches I had booked, so far, extended over a period of fourteen months and the most I had scheduled in any single month was five, which experience had taught me was just about anyone's effective limit considering that the engagements were scattered from Miami to San Diego. However, I wanted to discuss that with Pat, in person, and let him decide. Although I was now actually receiving several phone calls each week from meeting planners inquiring about Pat's availability and fee, I reluctantly decided to lay off making any further commitments beyond those speeches already booked until we talked face-to-face.

Pat had returned to his small spread in Blessings, Montana, but we usually spoke at least every other day on the telephone so that I could give him the latest tally of bookings made. Although his speaking schedule was not going to shift into gear for two more months, he wasn't at all concerned. He said that between the commercials that were being shot he was also working on a new and very important project that required peace, quiet and privacy. Even his planned move to New York was now on hold until the new undertaking was completed. He would be back in Manhattan in ten days, he said, to meet with Ted & Margaret's people again, and we could talk about his schedule. He also said if I were nice to him he'd even tell me about his special project.

And so, for the second time, Patrick Donne and I, at his request, jogged around Central Park soon after sunrise, only this time he came upstairs with me after we had completed our run and devoured at least a dozen of Mary's special blueberry pancakes to her great joy. After the kitchen table had been cleared, Mary poured a second cup of coffee for Patrick and me and then left us, saying, "Bart, I'll be upstairs for a while at the Wilsons. Joan has got to be at her bank this morning at ten and I promised I'd stay with Kathy. I shouldn't be more than an hour or so and Pat, in case you're gone when I get back down here, let me give you a hug now."

After Mary had left the room I said, "Kathy Wilson is a precious little nine-year-old who has spent the last three years or so in a wheelchair. She was hit by a cab right outside this building and her spinal cord was injured enough to paralyze the little sweetheart from the waist down. She loves Mary, and the two often go shopping together."

Patrick shook his head in admiration. "You are married to a very special woman, Bart."

154

"I know. And I also represent a very special speaker. Let's talk about him. I need to know how you feel about the number of speeches you can give each month. As you know, I've stopped booking until I know your feelings on the matter. If I keep making my phone calls and they keep calling me, who knows how many we can line up. What's your feeling?"

Pat sipped slowly on his coffee and exhaled deeply. "Let's set our limit at six a month."

"Six it is."

"Don't you want to know why I've decided on six?"

"Doesn't matter. If that's what you want, that's what you'll get."

"Bart, our fee is twenty thousand, right?"

I nodded.

"And your commission is twenty-five percent . . . five thou, right?"

Again I nodded.

"That leaves me with fifteen thousand dollars per speech. Six speeches per month is ninety thousand, and if we multiply that by twelve months, I will earn more than a million dollars per year. I cannot even imagine anyone making a million dollars in just twelve months, but that's now my goal."

"So you'll have more to give away?"

"I don't give it away. I just make a few investments in people. No big deal. There's an old saying that tells us we are rich only through what we give and poor only through what we keep. Any kind of charity is just a little love in action, that's all."

"Okay, we'll set the maximum number of speeches per month at six. Any exceptions?"

"I can be as flexible as necessary. If something special comes up, just call me and we'll deal with it. I'll also want to squeeze in some fund-raising appearances for charity whenever we can. No charge, of course."

"Done. Now . . . tell me about this new special project of yours."

Several minutes passed before he responded. "Well, as I've told you, Bart, I've been giving speeches now for about seven years . . . perhaps a couple of hundred in all. I love what I do and I truly believe I'm good at it, but I'm not convinced that we public speakers have as strong an effect on our audiences as many of us would like to believe. Several years ago I remember reading an article in *Disclosure* magazine that was very disturbing to me. A brilliant physician and educator with a long list of credentials, whose name I cannot recall, had written a provocative piece on learning in which he had stated that most of us are able to remember only ten percent of what we hear, ten minutes after we hear it. Well, I just didn't want to believe that most of the powerful points I thought I was making on the platform were going down the drain undigested, so I decided to quiz some of the members of several of my audiences almost immediately after my speech about the principles of success that I had covered. To my horror, the majority of those I asked actually couldn't recall much more than ten percent or so of all I had shared with them. Oh, they all said they had enjoyed the speech and I had fired them up to do better and they were certainly glad they had come, but when it came to specifics, they just mumbled things and tried not to look embarrassed."

Pat sipped his coffee, placed the half-empty cup in the

saucer and stared down at it. "I was pretty upset at what I had discovered and decided to kick it around with an old Montana friend, John Curtiss, who had been a high school principal in Billings before he retired to ski, read and play golf at the Red Elks Golf Club, where he and I played together quite often. We were sitting around, gabbing, one afternoon after he had whipped me pretty good on the course and I asked him, considering all his years of teaching, what he thought about that ten-percent theory that was really troubling me. He pondered for a while and then nodded his head, saying that it sounded about right. He was pretty certain, although he had never tried it, that if one read a chapter out of a history book to a ninth-grade class and then tested them on it, they would not score anywhere near as well as another ninth-grade class where you handed out books and asked them all to read that same chapter to themselves before testing them.

"Bart, I guess that what I remember most vividly is what John then taught me about Abraham Lincoln. He said that when Lincoln spoke at the dedication of the battlefield at Gettysburg, following famed orator Edward Everett's long speech, Abe's brief remarks attracted little if any attention. Lincoln, himself, was certain that his appearance and words had been a failure and a total waste of time. Later, however, when Lincoln's words were printed, they were acclaimed around the world . . . as they still are today, a hundred and thirty years later.

"Bart, after learning about my all-time hero, Lincoln, I did some research on my own—with all of it leading to the same conclusion—that the printed word somehow imbeds itself much more permanently on our brain than the spoken word.

Benjamin Franklin was an authentic genius and an excellent orator, but his wisdom and philosophy for a good life were taught to the world through his *Autobiography* and *Poor Richard's Almanac*. Napoleon Hill gave motivational speeches for years, but not until his 'steps to riches' appeared in print was he able to sell his ideas to millions. Norman Vincent Peale delivered his stirring sermons from the pulpit of his Marble Collegiate church, here in the city, for many years, but he reached national stature only after his thoughts on positive thinking appeared in print. Same with Dale Carnegie. The man was teaching night classes at the YMCA until *How to Win Friends and Influence People* was published. I am now absolutely convinced that messages delivered orally, no matter how powerful and dynamic, either in person or on tape, just do not compare in their power of retention with the printed word that one can read, reflect on, review . . . again and again."

"That special project. You're writing a book?"

Pat shook his head and smiled. "No, I'm trying to do something even more difficult."

"More difficult than writing a book . . . ?"

"I believe so. In a book you are free to use as many words as you believe you need to fully deal with your subject before moving on to the next chapter. What I'm trying to do is take those old and even ancient rules for a good life that I share with my audiences and convert them to a minimum of words and sentences that hopefully could be reproduced on a single piece of paper or cardboard. The fewer words the better, which is where the difficulty lies. This collection of wise advice, in whatever form I finally shape it, is going to be my special gift to everyone who hears me speak. Sometime toward the end of my speech I'll mention the small surprise they will all be receiving from me as they leave and then I'll ask them all to grant me one small favor. . . . "

I waited, saying nothing.

"Bart, I'm going to ask them all to read my little gift each morning before they start their day. I want them to get into the proper frame of mind to deal with the hours ahead, with all their challenges and pitfalls, temptations and dangers. I want them to follow my very simple road map along a path of life that will become much easier if they heed my advice, and if I can accomplish that goal, if I can affect more lives with assistance from the printed word, then so be it."

"And how is the project coming?"

He shook his head and sighed wistfully. "Very slowly. I don't even have a title for it yet, but I'm gaining. It's so easy to talk for twenty minutes about a secret of success, but it's very tough to write meaningfully about that same secret in just a twelve-word sentence. But . . . I'll make it. Should have it completed and printed before we really get rolling with our speeches."

Suddenly Pat reached into his side pants pocket, removed a key and placed it on the table in front of me. "Bart, what I'm working on is in a black looseleaf notebook in the top drawer of my old oak desk at my shack in Blessings. If anything should even happen to me before I get it finished and printed, I'd like you to have it to share with others, if you wish. Okay?"

Before I could respond, I heard Mary's voice in our hall fol-

lowed by childish laughter and the now-familiar squeak of a
wheelchair before Kathy Wilson appeared in our kitchen
doorway, followed by Mary.

"Hi, Mr. Manning!"

"Hi, Kathy. How's my pretty girl?"

"Fine."

"Kathy, this is Mr. Donne. He's our new friend."

"I know. Mrs. Manning told me." Kathy turned toward
Pat, who was now standing. Her left arm gently cradled a
smiling teddy bear wearing a golden crown adorned with red
jewels, gold lamé pants, a regal cape of soft purple velvet and
matching velvet slippers. She placed the stuffed bear in her
lap and rolled her wheelchair closer to Pat. Then she hastily
ran her small hand over her long blond hair before extending
it toward him and saying softly, "I'm very pleased to meet
you."

"How do you do, Kathy," Pat replied as he leaned down to
take her hand. "What's the name of your bear?"

"He's Prince Patrick, but I just call him Pat."

"Well, my name is Pat, too, and I'm really just a big bear
myself. Is Pat here your best friend?"

Kathy nodded shyly. "Yes he is, after God and my mom and
dad."

"What's that yellow tag hanging from his collar?"

"It says 'Pat, I love you.' I printed it myself and then signed
my name, Kathy, underneath. See!"

"Well," Pat replied, "I want you to know that I think both
you and your prince are very special."

The child suddenly extended both her tiny arms upward,
and Pat leaned closer until the fingers of her hands were

160

clasped tightly behind his neck. When the two finally separated, Pat kissed her softly on her forehead, lightly tapped both her knees with his fingers and said, "Be of good comfort, child."

There were tears in his eyes.

XVI

Mary reentered the kitchen wearing a light jacket and carrying her purse. "Bart, while I was upstairs Joan phoned and said that she was going to be tied up at the bank a lot longer than she expected, so Kathy and I are going out and doing some shopping. Should be back by noon."

"Okay. I'll be at the office all day. Now that Pat and I have worked out our numbers, I've got my work cut out for me. See you later, Kathy."

"So long, Mr. Manning. Bye, Mr. Donne." Kathy kissed the palm of her small right hand and waved it at both of us.

After they had gone, I turned to Pat, who was now sitting with his head lowered, both hands almost covering his coffee cup. "Are you okay?"

He glanced up, smiling wistfully. "I'm fine, just fine. Was just sitting here soaking in the atmosphere and special ambiance, if you will, of a real, honest-to-God kitchen that is lived in by people who love each other. Brought back memories of my mom and dad. I can still hear him cussing as he noisily loaded up our wood stove while Mother was trying to fry eggs and bacon in a giant black skillet. Memories, memories, memories . . ."

I patted Patrick Donne on the shoulder and said, "Don't you think it's about time you found someone to share a real nice kitchen with you along with that million-dollar income? Making any progress on that front?"

"Haven't had much time to look. It will all happen, not to worry. Are you going to the office today?"

"As soon as I shower, shave and get dressed."

"Walking?"

I nodded.

"Then I'll wait for you, if you don't mind. Keep you company. My morning is free."

"How long does Ted & Margaret's have you in the city this time?"

"All week. I'll be at the Plaza until next Monday, then back to Blessings for two uninterrupted weeks on my project."

When we finally arrived at my office, I invited Pat up but he said he had wasted enough of my time. That day, putting aside my mailing list and working on the names of meeting planners who had phoned me about hiring Pat that Grace had compiled, I made three firm bookings and two others said they would get back to me within the week.

On the following day I booked Pat two more times before noon, and after hanging up from making the second booking I strutted out into the outer office and saw Grace smirking at me.

"Did you say that you and Patrick had decided that his limit per month would be six speeches?" she asked.

"You've got it."

"God, Bart, at the rate you're knocking them off, he'll be booked solid for the next two years by the end of the month. I can't recall that we ever booked speakers two years ahead."

"I don't think I ever have. Remember how upset Eric used to get whenever I told him I had booked a speech for him even a year ahead?"

Grace grinned. "Yes, he would always ask us if we had some kind of a letter from God that assured us all that he would even be around in a year to give his talk."

"Well, two years is going to be our limit."

"What next . . . another speaker?"

"I don't think so. Not for a while, anyway. I'm enjoying this too much. No hassles. No struggles to make a sale. No fifteen phone calls back and forth to nudge someone to make up his or her mind. Hell, I don't even have to make a sales pitch to get this man a speaking date. Phenomenal!"

Grace nodded. "And those national commercials aren't hurting us any, that's for sure."

The phone rang. Grace lifted the receiver after the first ring and said sweetly, "Motivators Unlimited." She listened for a moment before saying, "He's right here." She waved the telephone receiver at me and said, "It's Mary."

I walked back into my office and picked up the phone. "Hi, hon."

"Bart, please come home right now!"

"What's wrong? You sound terrible. Talk to me. . . ."

"Everything is okay, but I still need you . . . now! And Patrick? Is he still in town? Try to get him, too. Please, darling.

Don't ask any questions. If you love me, just hurry home! And bring Patrick. Quickly. Please. . . ."

She hung up.

I phoned the Plaza and got lucky. As soon as Pat said hello I asked, "Do you have some free time right now?"

"Sure . . . what's wrong?"

"I don't know, Pat. Just received the strangest call I have ever had from Mary in all our years of marriage. She asked me to hurry home immediately and I was also to bring you, if possible. Will you come?"

"Of course."

"Okay, I'll grab a cab. You be out by the curb. Should swing by your hotel in less than ten minutes. Enough time?"

"I'm out of here," he said, and the phone went dead.

Our apartment door opened before I could insert my key in the lock. Mary's usually great complexion was ashen and her eyes looked as if she had been crying. When I took her in my arms she hugged me as if she were frightened and didn't want to let go. Her body was trembling.

"What's wrong, dear? For God's sake, tell me . . ."

"Nothing's wrong. You'll see. Patrick, thanks so much for being here. Now, come on into the living room, both of you."

Joan Wilson and her husband, Ted, were sitting quietly on our large sofa, holding hands and smiling. Next to the sofa sat Kathy in her wheelchair. When the child saw us, she dropped her teddy bear on her lap, waved both hands in our direction and said, "Hi, Mr. Manning. Hi, Mr. Donne."

In chorus we replied, "Hi, Kathy."

I turned to Mary. "Hon, what are you up to?"

She ignored my question. After introducing Pat to Ted and

Joan Wilson, she pointed to the two wing chairs directly across the room from where the Wilsons were sitting and said, "Bart, you and Pat sit there."

Pat looked at me and frowned. All I could do was shake my head and shrug my shoulders as we both took our seats obediently. Mary then walked to the center of our Persian carpet, directly under our chandelier, turned to Kathy and, sounding exactly like a bossy grammar-school teacher, asked, "Are you ready?"

Kathy smiled and nodded eagerly.

"Okay," Mary shouted, "do it!"

Kathy immediately placed the palms of both her hands on the wheelchair's two armrests. Then she inhaled deeply and pushed down with her arms. With the strain showing on her pretty face she gradually lifted her body from the chair and with the two foot supports turned upward, her feet slid downward until they were touching the floor. She continued pushing against the armrests until she was finally standing erect, her small and thin body swaying only slightly. Then she took a small step with her right foot, another with her left, then her right again, and she continued to step slowly and hesitatingly across the carpet, arms extended out from her sides as if she were trying to keep herself balanced on a tightrope. I'm sure we were all holding our breath. Finally, with a lunge she reached toward Pat and fell into his arms. She looked up at him and all of us heard her utter just two words—"Thank you!"

Late that night, long after Mary had turned off our bedroom lamp and cuddled up to my back, she asked, "Are you awake?"

"After this day, it's kind of hard to sleep," I replied slowly.

"I know. May I ask you one question . . . just one?"
"Shoot."
"Who is Patrick Donne?"
"Hon, I wish I knew."

In the months that followed, the speaking schedule I had been setting up for Pat gradually kicked into high gear and the man from Blessings soon found himself leading a far more hectic life than any he could have possibly imagined. Promoted, wherever he appeared, as the World Champion of the Lectern, Patrick Donne was one of the few speakers I ever knew who actually received standing ovations when he was introduced, and these same audiences, according to the reports received, always immediately settled down, becoming very quiet and attentive as soon as he commenced speaking. For sixty plus minutes Pat would share his dynamic and yet simple suggestions on how to live a happier and more productive life while he stood tall and compelling behind lecterns at the Anaheim Convention Center, the Boca Raton Resort and Club, Nashville's Opryland Hotel, the Arizona Biltmore in Phoenix, Boston's Hynes Convention Center, the Palmer Auditorium in Austin and the Wharton Center at Michigan State University to name only a few of the settings for his speeches.

The meeting planners who booked Pat, old friends and new contacts, represented corporations and organizations as varied as the auditoriums, ballrooms and hotels where he spoke. Some of his speeches, to audiences ranging in number from six hundred to more than eight thousand, were to United Consumer Club, the Association of Life Underwriters, Canada

Wide Magazine, Amway Corporation, Aim International, American Motivational Association, Alabama Association of Realtors, New Century Productions, Hill-Rom Corporation, Fruit of the Loom, Arbonne International, Re Max Real Estate, Ford Motor and yet he still managed to find time to do a fund-raiser for the Make-A-Wish Foundation in Phoenix.

Ten or fifteen years earlier, when Eric Champion and the rest of my speakers were at their peak, I had devised a system for meeting planners to rate the particular speaker they had employed. It was a very simple questionnaire with ten questions, each asking the meeting planner to rate the speech and the speaker on different qualities of the presentation from ten, "Absolutely magnificent," to zero, "Just plain lousy!"

Only once in all the years I represented Eric did he ever receive all tens. None of the others ever did. I had Grace resurrect the same rating system for Pat, and eight of his first twelve speeches from always tough-to-please judges gave Pat a perfect score! Five had even written on the comment lines beneath the questions that he had truly been the spellbinder I claimed he was!

In less than six months after his unforgettable evening at Trump Plaza for Latimer Investments, I had managed to book Pat solid, six speeches per month for the following two years except for both Decembers, when I could manage only one in each, which was no surprise or disappointment to either Pat or myself. Although the Ted & Margaret's commercials were coming to an end, Pat by now had become a familiar figure on national television, having appeared on all three morning network shows as well as "Donahue," "Regis & Kathie Lee," "Oprah Winfrey," "The Tonight Show" and a special with

David Frost, thanks to Terri and Vic's hard work. Whenever I called to compliment the two of them, Terri would always say that she wouldn't consider her work done until she had managed to get Pat on the cover of the *National Enquirer*. I was never sure whether she was kidding or not.

Pat was also honored by the Sales & Marketing Executives of Metropolitan St. Louis with the International Speaker's Hall of Fame Award, given to just one speaker each year, which was held by less than two dozen living Americans including such platform masters as Norman Vincent Peale, Bill Gove, Art Linkletter, Richard DeVos, Bob Richards and Cavett Robert, who had all been speaking to audiences for decades. Mary and I flew to St. Louis for that one, feeling very proud, and Pat's acceptance speech, when he paid homage to his late mother and father for instilling a dream of a better life in him, and me for helping him make it all come true, left very few dry eyes in the audience.

Pat and I continued to talk on the phone almost every day. He would phone from his hotel room if he had spoken on the previous evening, or from his home if he was between speeches. He would rate each of his speeches, using my system. He never gave himself a ten. Seven usually. Eight now and then. He always felt he could do better. Whenever he phoned from his home, I would also always ask him how his special project was progressing and he would tell me, as usual, that he was still struggling.

We didn't see much of each other for several months except for the few times when I had him booked in or close to Manhattan. I was constantly amazed, each time I heard him address a group, at how much he adjusted his speech for the

specific audience. The man did his homework. He would casually drop the names of high-level company executives, mention some of their corporate goals and didn't even hesitate to
name a product or plan that had bombed, although he did it in
such a manner that no one took offence. I was also fascinated
by the amount of practical wisdom that he shared, including
so many success principles that he had omitted because of the
time limitations at our speakers convention competition. Despite my love and respect for all my former speakers, I had to
admit that he was without a doubt the finest orator I had ever
heard, and yet there was not a single ounce of conceit in the
man!

Grace Samuels, as she had always done so expertly for all
my speakers of yesterday, made all the airline reservations for
Pat's trips through our longtime friend, Nancy McLaren at
Welcome Aboard, mailing first-class round-trip tickets to him
at least three weeks prior to each scheduled speech. Pat had
told her that he would prefer that she keep his commuter
flights on small planes to a minimum because they made him
uncomfortable, but every now and then it was unavoidable.
Months earlier I had booked him to do his thing at a convention of Bonham Distributors' top salespeople which was being
held at the lush Pilgrim Resort near Londonderry, Vermont.
For that one, although Grace tried her very best, it was going
to be necessary for Pat to fly into LaGuardia and then, five
hours later, catch a commuter for the small airport at Keene,
New Hampshire, where people from Bonham would meet him
and drive him to the Vermont resort. That Pat was going to
have five hours in Manhattan within a week was all Mary
needed to hear.

At breakfast the next morning she said, "Bart, I checked with Grace yesterday afternoon and she said that Pat would be arriving at LaGuardia at exactly four in the afternoon, next Thursday, and was scheduled to depart at nine. Joan Wilson gave me the good news at lunch yesterday that little Kathy has been recovering so swiftly from all her problems that she will begin attending public school again when they open in two weeks. The doctors still can't explain her complete recovery anymore today than they could when we saw her first push herself out of her wheelchair that day, but after all the private tutors and nurses for three years, the kid is finally going to re-join her old gang at school!"

"What great news!"

"Bart, I'd like to throw a small party for Kathy on Thursday. No big deal. Just her mom and dad and you and me and . . . Pat. Kathy is always talking about him and Joan says she keeps playing over and over on her Sony Walkman that tape you gave her of Pat giving his speech. If I scheduled the party for late afternoon when he's here in the city next Thursday, do you think he'd mind coming? He could check his luggage at LaGuardia when he arrives, grab a cab, spend a couple of hours with us, make it back to the airport and still catch his plane for . . . where is it . . . Keene? I know it would make one little girl very happy."

I leaned across the table and kissed her nose. "Only a little girl, huh?"

Of course Pat said he would come to the party, and he did, arriving shortly after five on Thursday, smiling and radiant as he thanked us again and again for inviting him. "You both make me feel like family. Kinda nice," he said as he hugged Mary.

"Well," Mary said, "if you feel like family, then you won't mind my putting you to work. Come with me!"

Pat followed her into the dining room, where the two of them spent the next thirty minutes placing all sorts of school material throughout the room. They put lunch boxes in several colors, rulers, pads of blank paper, several small slate blackboards, boxes of crayons and wooden pencils beneath scores of thin streamers of red crepe paper that Pat, with the help of a small stepladder, draped in long strips from one end of the room to the other on which he hung several paper replicas of old-fashioned school bells. "Mary," I heard Pat exclaim, "you should have been an artist, or at least an interior decorator!"

After a great spaghetti and meatball dinner, Kathy's favorite dish, Mary and Joan cleared the table. Within minutes, Mary reentered the living room carrying, on a silver tray, a large chocolate sheet cake shaped like an open book and decorated with a light cream frosting. On one of the full pages, in frosting, was the word "Kathy" and on the other page was the numeral "4" surrounded by four lit candles signifying, as Mary quickly explained, that we were celebrating Kathy's entrance into the fourth grade at the local public school.

After the large cake had been placed directly in front of Kathy, she leaned over without being told and blew out all four candles accompanied by loud applause.

"Did you make a wish, Kathy?" Pat asked, cocking his head in her direction.

"I did but I'm not going to tell. When you blow out candles and make a wish and tell, it never comes true."

We sat at the table, talking, laughing, joking and even

singing two verses of "School Days" before Pat looked at his watch and said sadly, "I'm sorry, everyone, but I've got to leave this nice party. Duty calls. First, however, will all of you just stay put for a couple of minutes? I've got to get something out of the coat closet in the hall."

When Pat returned he was carrying a box wrapped in gold foil. He handed it to Kathy, saying, "Here's a friend who will always stand by and watch over you."

Kathy looked up at Pat and smiled, softly stroking the shiny paper.

"Look, Mom!" she exclaimed. "This little gold sticker on the wrapping says 'Neiman . . . er . . . Neiman-Marcus.' "

Pat smiled. "When I saw it in the store window in Dallas last week I knew it was for you, and that was even before I had been invited to your party."

Kathy ripped at the paper, opened the cardboard box, removed several sheets of white tissue paper and there was a lovely angel almost a foot in height. Her gown was a lustrous rosy pink and cranberry velvet trimmed with gold and satin rosebuds. Behind her tiny upraised hands were wings of gold, and a small halo surrounded her prim porcelain face.

"See," said Pat, pointing to a small card attached to her tiny bejeweled belt, "her name is Kathy . . . and underneath her name I printed 'I love you' and signed it, 'Pat.' "

Kathy held the small angel close to her face and squealed. "Thank you so much! I love her! I'll put her in my bedroom so she'll be close to me and I can always talk to her whenever I feel sad or lonely."

"Sounds good," Pat said, kissing Kathy on the forehead. "Now give me a hug, because I've got to go."

When Kathy released Pat there were tears running down her cheeks. She turned to her mother and said, "Mom, can I please talk to you in the other room before Pat goes away?"

"Sure," Joan replied, and she immediately went out into the hall with Kathy following. Soon Joan returned alone, saying, "Pat, I'm sorry, but can you please wait just two more minutes? Kathy has something upstairs in her room that she wants you to have."

"What's she up to?" her father asked, but Joan just raised both hands, frowned at Joe and shook her head. Soon Kathy was back, out of breath, carrying Prince Patrick. She walked straight to Pat and held the stuffed bear out to him.

"Here," she said. "You gave me a pretty angel to watch over me but you have no mother or father or wife or . . . or child to take care of you. Prince Patrick will. Just remember to call him Pat and he will be your friend forever. I showed you this before, the card hanging from his neck, remember? It says 'Pat, I love you.' And I signed it, see, 'Kathy'!"

Pat glanced indecisively at Joan, but she was nodding faintly. Only then did he reach out and take the regal teddy bear gently in his two hands, touching the bear's lustrous gold crown softly against his cheek. "What a very special gift. I will guard him well, Kathy, and give him love. Thank you so much. What a wonderful present. Are you sure . . . ?"

"It's not even enough. You made me walk again."

"Well, I'm very touched, Kathy. Prince Patrick, I mean Pat, will remain my close friend forever. God bless you."

"God bless you, too," she said, falling into his arms for a final hug.

When Pat finally released Kathy and straightened up, he

said quietly, "Mary, do you have a fairly rugged shopping bag? I know there isn't any spare room in my luggage, so I'm going to carry my new buddy, the prince, on the plane with me up to New Hampshire. And when I return home to Blessings, Kathy, I'm going to place him on a special shelf that is right above the headboard of my bed, where we can be close to each other, okay?"

Kathy's eyes opened wide. She nodded and smiled.

Then she reached up as Pat stooped over and held her angel close to Pat's cheek to give him a farewell kiss.

XVII

Our bedroom phone is on Mary's side of the bed. We were both awake by its third jangling ring. I lay in the darkness, heard Mary lift the phone from its cradle and mumble "Hello."

I could hear a man's deep voice talking. Mary turned on her bedside lamp and sat up in bed. Then she placed her hand on my shoulder and said, "Dear, someone in New Hampshire wants to talk with you . . . a Sam Harding."

Sam Harding? Sam Harding? Then I remembered. He was the meeting planner at Bonham Distributors who had booked Pat for his keynote speech in Vermont. Sam had confirmed with me only last week that he would personally meet Pat's plane when it arrived at the Keene, New Hampshire, airport.

I glanced at my alarm clock. It was slightly after two in the morning. Then I took the phone from Mary and said, "Hi, Sam, what's wrong?"

I heard no response.

"Sam . . . Sam . . . are you there? This is Bart."

"I'm here, Bart, but I don't know how to say this now that I've got you on the line." I heard a soft moan.

"What's wrong? For God's sake, tell me! What happened? Did Pat miss the damn plane?"

Sam's voice broke. "I wish he had, Bart. We've been here, at the airport, since ten, waiting for his arrival even though the area is covered by a very dense fog, because they had told us the plane was in the air. We have just learned . . ."

"What . . . what??"

"Pat Donne's commuter plane crashed into the side of Little Monadnock Mountain at just around eleven o'clock. When it hit the mountain it exploded in flames. By the time the police and fire department from nearby North Richmond could even get close to the impact site, there was nothing remaining of the plane but a small pile of smoldering ashes . . . nothing!"

XVIII

My United Airlines flight from Denver arrived at Logan Field in Billings exactly on time, and when I entered the airport terminal building I had no difficulty recognizing John Curtiss. During the last of our three telephone conversations that had been held over the months since Pat's death, I told him I thought I was finally ready to come to Montana. He said he'd be proud to come pick me up at the airport and drive me to Pat's little place in Blessings and that he would be the old boy waiting for me at the gate who looked like Santa Claus in civilian clothes.

John Curtiss was certainly at least my age, but he plucked my clumsy suitcase from the luggage carousel as if it were a small paper bag. I followed the big man obediently out to the parking lot. As we were driving away from the airfield, he said, "Mr. Manning, I sure hope you don't mind riding in my old Chevy pickup. I've lived with this tough old gal for a ton of years and I just can't bring myself to part with such a good faithful friend."

"Hey, I don't mind at all. She's a lot more comfortable than any Manhattan cab I've been in for the last five years. And please call me Bart."

He turned and glanced at me approvingly, nodding his head with its wide-brimmed old Stetson tilted slightly forward but still not hiding his white, bushy eyebrows. "Bart, I'm sure glad you finally decided to come. I realize how tough all this is because I do believe I know how much that young guy meant to you . . . and how much you meant to him. He talked about you all the time. Said you were a nice man as well as the greatest agent in the country. I do believe that if you told him to go give his speech on top of our Grasshopper Glacier out here, he'd probably do it. That's why I kept phoning you. I'm sorry I was such a damn pest."

I reached over and patted his broad shoulder. "No apology needed, John. I did promise Pat, more than once, that if anything happened to him I'd come out here and retrieve his project in person. Thanks to you, I'm keeping my promise."

"Soon after he signed on with you, Bart, he came to me looking and acting very intense and announced that he was going to start making a lot of money. Since he had no living relatives, he wanted me to be his estate's executor in a will he was about to have drawn up. I couldn't say no. Besides showing me where he kept his checkbook and bankbook and the folder with his mutual fund stuff, he reviewed with me, again and again, the need for my getting in touch with you if anything ever happened to him. I was to make every attempt to work out whatever arrangement would be necessary in order to get you out here so that you could take possession of something special he was writing that he kept in the top unlocked drawer of his old desk in a black notebook. Said you already knew all about it. When I asked him why he didn't keep it in a safety deposit box in one of the two banks in Red Lodge along with his will if he considered it that important, he said he couldn't because the project wasn't completed yet. I can remember asking him whether it wouldn't be a lot simpler if I just took whatever he had in that drawer and mailed it directly to you in case anything ever happened, but he wouldn't buy that. He didn't give any reason, just said you had to come get it. You know, Bart, I never could bring myself to ask what exactly was in the drawer, and he never told me. Then, of course, I spent a lot of time in his house at his desk after we received the terrible news, trying to clean up his few bills, deal with the many charities he contributed to regularly and wrap up his other financial dealings, which were few. Yet never once, as God is my witness, did I so much as take a peek into that damn top drawer of the desk to see what was so almighty important . . . although I sure was tempted."

"When we get there, I'll show you. Somehow I don't think Pat would mind."

"Well, as I was saying, I'm mighty glad you finally decided to come. You probably didn't know this, sir, but you had a deadline. Pat had instructed me that if anything ever happened to him and I contacted you about coming out here to pick up that mystery package and you still hadn't made the trip a hundred and fifty days after his death, then I was to figure that God did not think very much of his effort. After I had notified the electric company to come turn off the power, I was to torch the place and just walk away from it, although I could first remove whatever I wanted. He even gave me those instructions in writing so that I wouldn't get in trouble with the authorities. You were getting mighty close to that dead-line, my friend. Nine days from now, as I reckon."

"Well, I thank God that I made it in time. I would have come sooner, but I went through my own little hell trying to deal with losing him. I've lost speakers and close friends many times through the years, but none hurt like this one. Patrick was the son I never had. He also had an incredible gift on the platform. They called him a spellbinder . . . and he was. Al-though the newspapers, radio and television were filled with the news of the tragedy for weeks, I still felt it my duty to call every meeting planner who had booked Pat for a future speech and every one of those conversations drove another spike into my heart. Then I got roped into a lot of interviews with re-porters wanting to know what Patrick Donne was really like. John, I can remember Pat telling me that you were a teacher and high school principal. Did you ever have him in any of your classes?"

"Sure did . . . grades seven through nine."

"So what was he like as a kid?"

"Pat was a big boy for his age, but he never used his size or muscle to bully the other kids, only to break up their fights. He was also very quiet. A good student. No problems in or out of class. Loved animals and was always taking care of one or two stray dogs or cats that no one wanted. I remember he once tended a tiny bear cub for weeks after rescuing him from a deep crevasse in the mountains. One summer he also saved a little boy who was drowning in a pond near Red Lodge, and he was constantly running errands for old folks. A very special kid. My wife often said that he was practicing to grow up to be

a saint, because he was always so filled with love for everyone
. . . for all living things."

"He told me that you two played a lot of golf together."

"Well, we did until you started sending him all over the
country. Yeah, we played a lot and I'm pretty certain that he
usually let me beat him. That would be Patrick, never thinking of himself so long as he could make someone else feel a little better about life."

We rode along in silence for several minutes before John
raised his arm and pointed at the panorama of craggy mountain beauty unfolding before us. "So what do you think of Big
Sky country?"

"Awesome. Flying up from Denver, I thought that this must
be what heaven looks like."

"We've been climbing a bit on this fine piece of federal
highway since we left Billings, but we should be at the town of
Red Lodge in about forty minutes. South of Red Lodge is what
they call the Beartooth Range of the Rockies. In the summer
months when it is open to traffic, the Beartooth highway will
give you a mind-blowing entrance into Yellowstone National
Park as you drive on roads engineered high into the mountains
among glacial lakes and arctic tundra. Granite Peak is also in
the Beartooths, and it's the highest mountain in our state at almost thirteen thousand feet. Red Lodge, my home for a lot of
years, is a great place to live. No humidity, no mosquitoes.
Never gets much above eighty in the summer and, at night,
even in August, you usually still have to sleep under a blanket."

Soon after we had passed through Red Lodge, with its wide
main street and countless stores displaying everything from
cowboy boots and Levi's to bathing suits and television sets,

we turned east at a small sign which read 308 and listed the names of four towns—WASHOE, BEARCREEK, BLESSINGS, BELFRY. John's old Chevy began to buck and sway as he struggled to keep it on course on the narrow, rutted dirt road. On both sides were green pastures as far as the eye could see. Cattle grazed everywhere, and on the horizon were more jagged mountain peaks, some still covered with snow.

John pointed ahead again, through his windshield. "Around ninety miles northeast of here George Custer ran into a lot more trouble than he was expecting back in 1876."

"Little Big Horn?"

"Yup. If you stand on that long sloping hill where Custer and his men made their last stand, I swear you can still hear yells and screams and shots being fired. There are a lot of gravestones there where some of the men were buried right where they had fallen. Now, New York man, I'm pretty sure you didn't even notice that we've already passed through the townships of Washoe and Bearcreek. Somewhere along here, on the right, is the big ranch that Pat's mother and father ran for so long. There, see that big clapboard house under all those red cedar trees? That's where our guy grew up. As you know, he sold all this land, except for a few acres, when his mother passed on and he decided he wanted to be a full-time public speaker instead of a rancher."

John leaned on his horn as we passed the driveway of what had been Pat's ranch, and several children as well as a couple of grown-ups turned and waved. Another young man in overalls who was driving a tractor in a huge yard on the side of the house looked up and tipped his baseball cap at John's obviously recognizable old red pickup.

In a few moments we turned left on an even narrower dirt road, this one flanked on both sides by pine trees so near that their lower branches rubbed against the side of John's truck as we went past. Suddenly we were in a small clearing on which sat a log cabin with a steeply sloped roof. At the rear of the cabin was some sort of storage shed over which hovered an ancient gnarled but still-leafy apple tree.

John parked and said nothing.

"Is this it?" I asked.

He nodded.

"Pat always referred to the place as a three-room cottage."

"Well, it does have three rooms—a small bedroom, a kitchen with an old wood stove and a living room with a fireplace that was also Pat's office—at least that's what he called it. That storage shed is where he kept his Harley before he sold it."

As I was opening the truck door John said, "You know, Bart, I plumb forgot to ask you what your plans were for tonight."

"Well, I just thought I'd spend the night in some hotel in Billings and then fly back to New York in the morning. My plane leaves for Denver at ten-fifteen."

"Sounds fine. You've got your key for this place, right? Pat said he gave you one."

I reached into my pocket and nodded.

"Good." He chuckled. "If it's okay with you, I'll just leave you to your business inside there, kind of let you mingle with Pat's presence, if you believe in that sort of thing. I've got a couple of errands to do in Red Lodge and then I'll come on back and pick you up and get you to a hotel in Billings. An hour okay?"

"Just so long as you come back, John. I don't know how well I'd survive out here."

He laughed. "Not to worry. Pat would never forgive me if I deserted you." He glanced at his wristwatch. "Four o'clock okay?"

"Perfect. John, I can't thank you enough for all this."

"Hey, you're a nice guy, Bart, but I'm not doing this for you. I'm just following Pat's orders. See you at four."

I watched as he backed the truck down the driveway. Then he rolled down the side window, stuck his head out and shouted, "Before I depart, let's be certain your key works, what do you say?"

I walked up to the faded blue wooden door and turned the key. I heard a soft click and then, with a little pressure, the door opened inward. I turned and waved at John as he gunned the truck's motor and roared down the dusty roadway.

The interior walls of the cabin were of rough, unfinished boards stained in a rust tone that gave the cluttered room an almost iridescent glow. I closed the door softly, feeling very strange and uncomfortable, as if I were in the presence of something I couldn't comprehend. Directly across from where I was standing was a large battered oak desk and an old swivel chair with a tattered pad on its seat. Stacked neatly on each side of the desk were several large plastic boxes in various colors, filled with file folders. To the right of the desk was a natural stone fireplace. I walked very tentatively toward it. The half-burned remains of a log were still in the grate, and above a thick wooden mantel hung a large, brass-framed reproduction of Dürer's "Praying Hands." On the mantel was an oval photo of a stern and unsmiling man and woman in sepia tone, probably Pat's mom and dad, and next to it was a photo of a young man in a football uniform posing awkwardly as he held his helmet against his thigh. There was no doubt it was Pat.

Every interior wall was alive with vivid colors from scores of hanging rugs, and stacked against each wall were piles of books. Next to a small twelve-pane window that looked out on the nearby woods hung several bridles, a small saddle and a piece of needlepoint depicting an Indian brave. On the other side of the desk was a cane sofa that looked completely out of place and an armless wooden rocker. A coffee table piled high with magazines was in the center of a large, oval braided rug that nearly covered the entire living room. The only sound I could hear was the wind blowing outside. Here was a magical place where anyone could have lived and shed all the tensions of life. A blessed retreat. An enchanted haven. I could almost feel Pat's presence. I think it was Pascal who once wrote that most of our misfortunes spring from not knowing how to live quietly at home, in our own rooms. The place fitted Patrick Donne perfectly. That a man who loved life as much as he did and knew how to live so well had to die so young was totally unfair. And far beyond me.

Adjoining the large room was a tiny open kitchen containing a cast-iron stove and a circular wooden table with several unmatching chairs. On a small end table next to the stove was an old-fashioned wooden radio and a glass jar filled with hard candy.

I moved slowly toward the closed door to my left and opened it just wide enough to see the bottom half of a bed covered by a rust and gold quilt. I couldn't bring myself to enter, so I quickly pulled the door shut, turned and walked back

toward the desk. Even sitting in Pat's old swivel chair I felt uncomfortable. A black notepad and an old telephone were the
only objects on the desk. I lifted the receiver to my ear and
heard the familiar dial tone. How many times had Pat talked
with me on this telephone? Was it during our final conversation, before he came east for the last time, when he had
proudly announced that he thought his special writing project
was finally completed? "Bart," I can still hear that commanding voice announcing, "I do believe I'm ready to take my little
effort public. I'm going to have a printer friend in Red Lodge
lay it out and then set the thing in two or three different styles
and sizes of type and then I'll select one. Sure hope you like it.
I don't know how many wastebaskets I have filled, over the
months, trying to create a special but brief document that
could change lives for the better. I truly believed my idea had
merit, but it just wouldn't go down on paper in a way that satisfied me. I finally got so confused that I scuttled all my notes
and went back to ground zero, setting just two criteria for my
work. It had to be a code of life that could be read in no more
than five minutes each morning, so that the principles of success would easily and quickly imbed themselves in one's conscious and subconscious for the day. Also, it had to be the
same advice I would give a son or daughter who came to me
pleading for guidance on how to achieve a life of success, pride
and peace of mind while avoiding all the sorry traps of failure.
What I ended up with was pretty close to what I told you I had
started with several months ago—the most powerful principles
that I use in my own speeches, each condensed to as few words
as possible."

I remember holding the phone and listening, saying not a

word as he continued. "Bart, as soon as I decided that the advice I wanted to give the world was exactly what I would share
with those I love, everything seemed to fall into place. I just
sat down the other night and started writing on a legal pad,
and the next thing I knew it was dawn, and although there
were a lot of crumpled balls of yellow paper on the floor, my
project was done . . . and even I was satisfied. Amazing! I don't
remember writing any of it. When I timed myself it took just a
little under five minutes to read. Perfect! I'd like to distribute
copies to everyone attending my future speeches so that it
won't matter if they remember only ten percent of what I say
so long as they have a daily reminder of some of the most important principles. At no charge, of course. Later I'm certain
that between you and me we'll be able to figure how to get the
message into the hands of many others who are hoping and
praying, right now as we talk, for someone to throw them a
lifeline."

There was a long pause. I remember waiting, again saying
nothing. "Bart, we've got a world of hurting people who seem
to have lost all faith in themselves and others. I believe that
conditions are far worse now than they were fifty or a hundred
years ago. So many just cannot cope and so they quit. They
crawl into a hole and spend the rest of their days hiding in despair while others strike out in terror and panic and often end
up bringing pain and even death to their fellow man. We cannot allow this world to continue on its present downward
path. You and I may be only two wanderers on the beach of
life, but we can make a difference to many. I truly believe
that! Oh." He chuckled. "If you wonder where I got the title
for my project, all I'll tell you for now is some of it came off the

cover of an old model airplane kit box that I found in the shed the other day. Go figure . . ."

But now Patrick Donne was dead and it was all in my hands. I inhaled deeply and pulled open the long, narrow front drawer of his desk. The old black notebook was right where he had said it would be. I removed it gently from the drawer and placed it on the frayed crimson-colored desk pad. My hands were trembling. I looked up as I inhaled deeply and found myself staring at that memorable pair of praying hands above the fireplace. Then I shut my eyes, trying to get control of myself. The guttural hum of a commercial jet plane flying high overhead was the only sound I could hear except my own breathing. I took another deep breath, opened the notebook slowly and commenced reading. . . .

XIX

ASSEMBLY INSTRUCTIONS FOR YOUR NEW LIFE

You already possess all the tools and materials necessary in order to change your life for the better. In this world the greatest rewards of success, wealth and happiness are usually obtained not through the exercise of special powers such as genius or intellect but through one's energetic use of simple means and ordinary qualities.

Do not be deceived by the brevity of these instructions. Though they contain few words, they were all drawn from centuries of experience. Old seeds they may be, yet they are all filled with new life. Review them every morning before you begin your day. After they are planted in your heart they will grow into a wondrous garden of achievement and contentment that can be cultivated, admired and harvested as long as you live. . . .

Step One First, recognize that you are not a sheep who will be satisfied with only a few nibbles of dry grass or with following the herd as they wander aimlessly, bleating and whining, all of their days. Separate yourself now from the multitude of humanity so that you will be able to control your own destiny. Remember that what others think and say and do need never influence what you think and say and do. *Separate yourself from the crowd.*

Step Two As soon as you awake, seal yourself in a day-tight compartment so that you will live only for this day and its allotted work. Yesterday has vanished forever and tomorrow is only a dream. Refuse to allow painful memories of the past or hand-wringing concerns about tomorrow to befoul your thinking so that today's efforts are impaired. Get rid of both heavy loads, yesterday's and tomorrow's, so that you can advance swiftly today toward the good life you deserve. *Live each day in a day-tight compartment.*

Step Three Go the extra mile at every opportunity today and you will be following the greatest secret of success known to man. The one certain method of turning this day into a glorious success is to work harder, longer and more intensely than anyone expects you to do. Always render more and better service than that for which you are being paid and you will soon be paid for more than you do. *Go the extra mile!*

Step Four Realize that almost every adversity that may befall you today usually carries with it an equivalent or greater benefit that you will find if you have the courage to look. Collect your thoughts whenever you suffer a setback and ask yourself what possible good can be extracted from your misfortune. The scales of life always return to center, and if God closes one door to you, another will be opened. Never abandon hope. *Look for the seed of good in every adversity.*

Step Five Never neglect the little things. One of the greatest differences between a failure and a success is that the successful person will tackle chores that the failure avoids. Work done hastily, shortcuts taken, careless attention to details—these can all eventually wreak great havoc on your career. Constantly remind yourself that if it is part of your work, however small a task it may be, then it is important. History still reminds us of ancient battles that were lost because of a missing horseshoe nail. *Never neglect the little things.*

Step Six Never hide behind busy work. It takes just as much energy to fail as it does to succeed. You must constantly guard against the trap of falling into a routine of remaining busy with unimportant chores that will provide you with an excuse to avoid meaningful challenges or opportunities that could change your life for the better. Your hours are your most precious possession. This day is all you have. Waste not a minute. *Never hide behind busy work.*

Step Seven Live this entire day without allowing anyone to rain on your parade. The wounds to your inner self can be painful and long-lasting whenever anyone taunts or criticizes you. As you now begin to climb the golden ladder of success, you will constantly encounter those who will attempt to drag you down to their level. This has always been the way of the world, and if you permit it to happen to you, the pounding you receive will eventually cause you to cease your climb in order to avoid future pain. Just smile and walk away from it. Envy always implies the conscious inferiority of others. *Never allow anyone to rain on your parade.*

There are hundreds of other success laws and principles in the world, and most of them would probably help you advance toward the good life you seek. However, the seven you have just received, by themselves, have more than enough power, according to their past record, to make all your dreams come true if you will review them each morning and then apply them to the hours of your day.

As a wise man once wrote, realize that between your birth and your death the hours and the days and the years will probably be many. Yet there is no cure for birth, no cure for death, so you may as well be happy with your allotted interval and live it with pride, peace, honor, love and accomplishment. Follow just these few direct instructions every day and all that will definitely come to pass.

This very moment, through these pages, you have come to the crossroads of your life.

Your struggle has ended. God is nodding . . . and smiling.

XX

❦

I closed the notebook slowly and stared at it for I don't know how long. Finally I pushed myself back from the desk, tucked the notebook under my arm and stood. I glanced at my wristwatch. If Curtiss was true to his word, he'd be returning for me in about fifteen minutes. I decided to spend those final minutes outside, breathing in some pure, sweet-smelling country air, but as I was heading toward the front door I paused and glanced toward the closed door to my right.

Without hesitation this time, almost as if I were being drawn by some force I could not ignore, I walked directly toward Pat's bedroom, pushed the door wide open and stepped inside. An old-fashioned canvas window shade had been pulled all the way down so that very little light entered from the outside. I hit the light switch next to the doorway, turning on a small wooden urn-shaped lamp that sat on an unfinished dresser. Above the switch, in a tarnished pewter frame, was an aged piece of parchment on which, in distinctive calligraphy

were the words *Find something you love to do so much in your life
that you would be willing to do it for free—Bill Gove.*

A reflected image in the large dresser mirror almost caused
me to drop the notebook. Sitting on a shelf above the headboard of the single bed was a brown teddy bear, looking very
much like the one Kathy Wilson had presented to Pat, with
his golden crown, velvet cape, shining gold pants and purple
slippers. Typical of Pat, of course, was that he hadn't divulged
to little Kathy Wilson, on that ill-fated day when she had
proudly presented him with her teddy bear called Pat, to
watch over him, that he already owned one. I could still
vividly remember her saying that since he had given her a
pretty angel to watch over her and since he had no one to take
care of him, Prince Patrick would watch over him from then
on. I could even remember how Kathy had proudly shown Pat
the yellow card hanging from her teddy bear's neck on which
she had printed "Pat, I Love you" and then signed *Kathy* with
her own hand underneath the words. Later that afternoon, before Pat had left our apartment, he had asked Mary for a
rugged shopping bag of some sort so that he could carry his
new friend with him on the small commuter plane to New
Hampshire, since his luggage was all packed.

I moved closer to the head of the unmade bed, reached
out and gently lifted the teddy bear from the shelf, cuddling
him close to my face as if I were a child again, a lonely child.
"Pat . . . Pat . . ." I heard myself sobbing. "I sure do miss you!"

A yellow card hanging from the teddy bear's collar cut
sharply against my cheek. Remembering the card on Kathy's
Prince Patrick, I held the bear at arm's length so that I could
read the words on this one.

Dear God!

Dear God!

Printed in unevenly sized and spaced letters as a child would print were the words Pat, I Love you.

And beneath that precious declaration the card was signed . . .

. . . . *Kathy.*

ABOUT THE AUTHOR

Og Mandino is the most widely read inspirational and self-help author in the world today. His sixteen books have sold more than thirty-two million copies in twenty languages. Thousands of people from all walks of life have openly credited Og Mandino with turning their lives around and for the miracle they have found in his words. His books of wisdom, inspiration and love include *The Greatest Salesman in the World*; *The Greatest Salesman in the World, Part II: The End of the Story*; *The Christ Commission*; *The Greatest Secret in the World*; *Og Mandino's University of Success*; *Mission: Success!*; *A Better Way to Live*; and *The Return of the Ragpicker*.